P9-DCB-932

Landscapes & Illusions

Creating Scenic Imagery with Fabric
by Joen Wolfrom

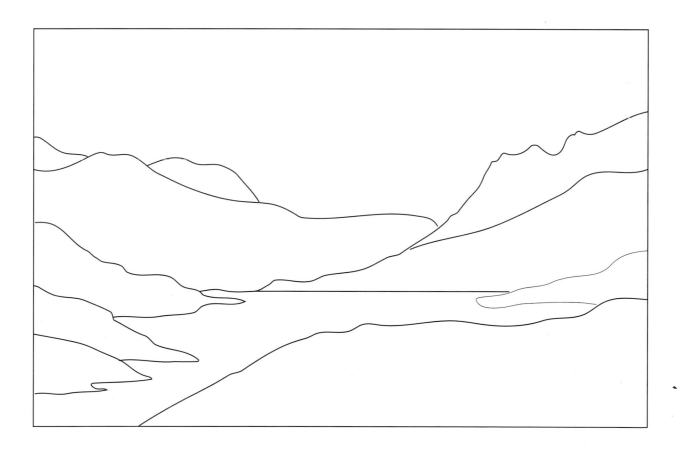

C&T PUBLISHING

Landscapes & Illusions
Creating Scenic Imagery with Fabric
Copyright © 1990, Joen Wolfrom
2nd printing 1991

Front Cover Photo:
Serenity At Dawn by Joen Wolfrom
Private owner, Finland
Back Cover Photo:
View From My Childhood Garden by Joen Wolfrom
From the Collection of Ulster Folk
and Transport Museum, Northern Ireland
All textile art by author was constructed on a 1971 Bernina Record 730

Editor: Nadene M. Hartley
Copy Editor: Judith M. Moretz
Design & Art Director: Diana L. Grinwis
Grinwis Art Service, East Lansing, Michigan. This project was produced on
an ARC 386 using Ventura Publisher 2.0 with Professional Extension software.

Illustrator: Jonathan Benallack
Windward Graphics, Lansing, Michigan. The illustrations were produced on
a MacIntosh Plus using Illustrator 88 software.

Published by
C & T Publishing
P.O. Box 1456
Lafayette, California 94549

ISBN 0-914881-32-9

All rights reserved. No part of this work covered by the copyright
hereon may be reproduced or used in any form or by any means—
graphic, electronic or mechanical, including photocopying, re-
cording, taping or information storage and retrieval systems
without written permission of the publisher.

The copyrights on individual works are retained by the artists as
noted in *Landscapes & Illusions*.

Library of Congress Catalog Card No: 90-62170

Printed in the United States

Pantone is a registered trademark of Pantone, Inc.
Fairfield Cotton Classic Blend is a registered trademark
of Fairfield Processing Corporation.

Table Of Contents

The Photo Gallery begins on page 26

Acknowledgments

I am deeply grateful to the people who have been directly responsible for bringing *Landscapes & Illusions—Creating Scenic Imagery with Fabric* to fruition. Thanks to Tom, Carolie, and Todd Hensley, whose interest inspired me to complete this manuscript. I wish to also thank the support staff of Diane Pedersen, Judy Moretz, Jonathan Benallack, and Diana Grinwis, whose suggestions, knowledge, expertise, and talents have combined to create a book that presents this subject matter in the best possible format. Special thanks goes to Nadene Hartley, whose valuable editing suggestions guided me immeasurably.

Additionally, I wish to thank Judith Buskirk, who gave me wise advice and insight during the writing of this manuscript, and to Janice Richards, who continues to share her fabrics and ideas with me. My appreciation goes to Diane Armstrong, Ann Bird, Erika Carter, Phyllis Danielson, Lorraine Doyle, Geraldine Gahan, Sally Glutting, Janine Holzman, Martie Huston, Carol Johnson, Jean V. Johnson, Pat Magaret, Marion Marias, Joanne Myers, Shirley Perryman, Judy Sacha, Marie Terhune, Signe Twardowski, Carol B. Wheeler, and Karen Wooten, who all agreed so graciously to share their beautiful art.

I also wish to acknowledge and thank those individuals who influenced me in their own unique ways during the years that preceded the final writing of this book. Their cumulative wisdom, encouragement, suggestions, support, and guidance have been instrumental in my growth as a quiltmaker, artist, and writer. So to you who have played a role, whether considerable or brief, I thank you very much: JoAnne Cross, Kathy Fields, Kathy Fina, Lynda Kelley, Bonnie Leman, Elly Sienkiewicz, DeLoris Stude, Lenore Watkins, Jean Wells, Diane Wolf, Essey Wolfrom, Sharon Yenter, and the WITS.

For friendship, support, and early opportunities, I wish to give special recognition to Dorothea Peterson. Her years of selfless giving and labors of love to preserve and promote Gig Harbor Peninsula's history and quilting interests will long be remembered by all who knew her and appreciated her quiet, thoughtful efforts.

I sincerely thank conference sponsors, organization members, educational faculties, editors, and individuals who have invited me to teach, lecture, write, and share my ideas and knowledge. These experiences challenged me to crystalize my thoughts. For those who have requested that I put my knowledge in print form, this book is especially for you.

This Book Is Dedicated

To
my three children
Danielle Renée, Dane Winslow, and David Daniel,
upon whom I wish to bestow
a priceless gift:
the steadfast belief in the abilities of oneself.
May they also inherit the wisdom of those before them.

To
my husband, Dan,
who believes that women have their own dreams to catch,
and who always believed that I could...

To
my father, Win,
who encouraged me to challenge myself,
to be curious, to think, to care,
to be committed to personal ideals,
to recognize when the doors of life were open,
and to then have the courage to walk through them
to meet the unknown.

To
my grandmother, Janey Crawford Stewart,
who taught me to love the beauty of our earth,
to look for the special qualities in each person,
to be positive in my attitude,
and to joyfully share, give, and love.

To
my homeland, Washington State,
whose 100th birthday is being celebrated
while I write this manuscript, and
whose breathtaking beauty and serene ambiance
have inspired me
to recreate its spectacular scenery in fabric.

Foreword:
The Birth Of An Idea

Currently we see a growing number of artists and quiltmakers experimenting with non-traditional fabric construction methods to create artistic statements using their own personal design and color styles. Happily, these innovative individuals and their artistic contributions are becoming a recognized and important part of the continuing growth in both art and quilt history. Additionally, the blending of historical influences with this evolving creative expression gives a refreshing balance to the total spectrum of both worlds. The result is an art form and craft which is diverse, exciting, strong, and in constant motion.

Diversity is spawned by people searching for new ideas and techniques to use when they find that established methods are not compatible with their desired goals. That is how I developed my particular technique for creating fabric landscapes. For several years I enjoyed creating whimsical appliquéd country scenes. Then, when I attempted to create more sophisticated landscapes through this technique, I found that the artistic effects I sought eluded me. I was disappointed that I couldn't accomplish in fabric what I envisioned in my mind.

At that time, I had to decide whether creating sophisticated fabric landscapes was a fleeting idea or an ardent creative passion that would resist being mentally discarded. When I realized that my mind was determined to resolve this technical design problem, the slow journey toward a solution began. I set about experimenting with plausible ways to create scenes that would aesthetically celebrate the beauty of our natural environment. Eventually, through trial and error, I devised a method to accomplish the desired effect.

Almost a decade has passed since my quest began. I have enjoyed creating my own interpretations of the world while playing with a unique palette of fabrics. Upon reflection, this seems the right time to take a creative pause, to pull together my ideas, discoveries, observations, and learnings, and to share this collection of information with you. Thus, *Landscapes & Illusions—Creating Scenic Imagery with Fabric* is now in your hands.

I invite you to use this book to help build a basic foundation of color, design, and techniques for creating beautiful fabric landscapes. To use this book most effectively, read the complete text, chapter by chapter, digesting each one's information thoroughly before proceeding to the next. When you have finished reading, practice the techniques discussed in Chapter IX. Once those techniques have been learned, work through the lessons in Chapter X. These lessons include basic directions as well as suggestions for finding help, making modifications, and expanding what you have learned.

You can enjoy success in creating beautiful landscapes with no previous experience in formal art or quiltmaking. When creating these scenic pictures, the only prerequisites for success are a working knowledge of the sewing machine, a love of nature, a desire to learn, and the ability to persevere.

I hope that this book will guide you in your own exploration of creating landscapes, in your search for increasing your knowledge of color use and visual illusions, in your desire to use quilting lines to their optimum design potential, and in your quest to acquire new ideas and technical skills for creating future works of art.

PART ONE

The Visual Foundation

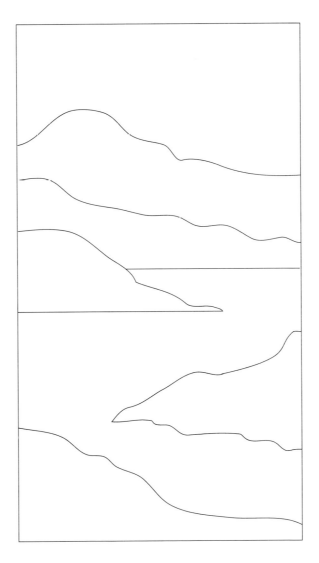

Chapter I
Using Color Naturally

Success in creating beautiful landscape pictures does not depend solely on construction techniques. Color is the primary element that attracts us to an artwork, and its use within a picture is of supreme importance. Consequently, we need to investigate and understand the use of color within landscape pictures before beginning the construction process.

Luckily for most of us, making a gorgeous quilt or fabric art does not require years of experience at the sewing machine or the quilting frame. In fact, a novice technician who makes excellent color choices to enhance a good design can create a beautiful work of art while working to increase her skill level. When thoughtful color and design choices are combined with superb technical ability, the results can be quite dazzling.

Some people have an intuitive understanding of color. Most of us, however, need to work toward developing a personal color style. Individual likes and dislikes in color are formed in a complex manner by many influences. These can include the environment of our childhood, our current natural surroundings, past experiences, our peers and family, learned color associations, advertising, and current trends. Color understanding will develop more rapidly if we begin by working with hues that please us. As our comfort level rises, our ability to work with more colors increases.

During the beginning stages of color exploration, we usually have very little confidence in our own decision-making abilities. Through experimentation, we learn to trust our own intuition. This is an important step for each of us, because we are the only ones who can discover the colors which bring us our own emotive energy and personal joy. When we identify and use colors that inspire us creatively, the artwork reflects our inner self. Admittedly, it takes courage to rely on our own choices and to accept the natural mistakes which result from initial experimentation. But happily, we will be rewarded eventually for these efforts by finding the unique color personality that belongs solely to us.

COLOR SCALES

Because color is so essential to creating landscapes, a working knowledge of certain basic color principles is necessary. The ability to work with various color scales is the most important factor for success. Although you may not have had prior formal experience in this field, the color concepts used in landscapes are actually quite simple to understand. Subconsciously, you already know much of this information just from a lifetime of observing color in the world around you.

Color scales are very similar to musical scales. They simply give fundamental order to certain elements of color. The four color scales are pure hues, tints, shades, and tones, and each plays an integral part in setting the mood or timing of a picture. Also, the visual illusions of depth, luminosity, and luster are all achieved by working with one or more of these color scales. Because color scales will play such a prominent role in your work, you must know and recognize their differences.

Pure Colors

Primary colors and all hues formed by mixing primaries are pure colors. Pure colors are clear, vivid, and high in intensity. They translate into the strong colors of summer. If you plan to create a scene with a summer setting, the majority of your colors should come from the pure hues. Pure colors used in a landscape make a lively, vibrant visual impact.

Because pure colors have such strength, they should be used with great care in order to maintain visual balance. A pure color should not "pull out" without intent. For instance, an unchecked amount of yellow, the strongest pure color, can be visually distracting if it unintentionally takes on a dominant role. Use pure colors cautiously because visual balance supersedes physical balance.

Also be conscious of how pure colors interact with hues from other color scales. Do not let them overpower your design. Even though their strength can become a disadvantage if poorly placed, it can also be their most desired feature. Pure colors can set dramatic moods, create visual illusions, give zest, and add dazzle. When you want a visual outcome that can only be obtained with pure colors, let these vibrant hues bring out the best in your design.

In our study of color, we often see pure hues arranged around a circle, or color wheel. The pigment color wheel used by many artists is called the Ives Color Circle. When this pure color wheel is divided into twelve equal divisions, the colors include the three primary hues: yellow, cyan (turquoise), and magenta; the three secondary colors: green, violet, and orange; and the six intermediate colors: yellow-green, blue-green, blue, purple, red, and yellow-orange. Additionally, the color wheel can be broken into twenty-four colors, forty-eight colors, or even more divisions, if desired. All of the colors are obtained by continuing to blend the primary colors. (See Figure 1.)

Tints

The dramatic mood of pure colors is counterbalanced by the delicate nature of tints. Tints are colors which change from the pure form by having white mixed with them. Depending upon the amount of white added to the pure hue, the color can either be just a hint lighter than the pure color, so light that only a blush of the hue can be perceived, or somewhere between these two extremes. The most commonly recognized hues within the tint scale are the soft, delicate pastels.

The colors within the tint scale reflect the season of spring. They are light, airy, and very fragile. Their mood can be gentle. If you wish to create a spring scene, then choose the majority of your colors from the tint scale. The perfect neutral for these colors is white, because it exists within all tints. In addition to using tints for spring scenes, they are sometimes used to attain luster and luminosity.

Common tints and their root colors include: cream/yellow, pink/red, peach/red-orange or yellowish pink, apricot/orange or yellow-orange, lavender/purple or violet, mint green/green, robin's-egg blue/blue-green, and light blue/blue.

Shades

When pure colors are mixed with black, they become shades. With a small amount of black added, the color is only slightly darker than the pure hue; the more black added, the darker the color becomes. Some shades, like dark navy and eggplant, can seem almost black. Shades are always darker than the pure color. The most natural neutral to use with these colors is black, because it is present in all shades.

Figure 1. The Color Wheel

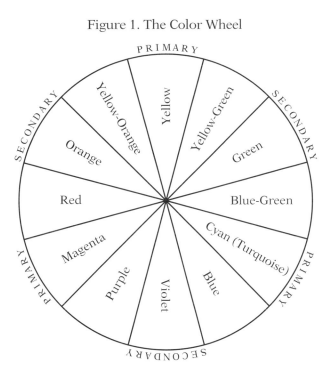

Emotionally, shades are rich and deep, and are naturally associated with autumn colors. If you want to create a picture that reflects a beautiful autumn day, your color choices will be primarily from the shade scale. (See photos 45 and 46.) Late evening landscapes also utilize shades. (See photo 42.) While working with visual illusions, shades are most often used for developing luster and they can also be used to develop shadows.

Common shades and their root colors include: olive/yellow; brown and rust/yellow-orange, or orange, or red-orange; maroon/red or purplish red; plum/purple or reddish purple; and navy/blue.

Brown and Rust

Two shades, brown and rust, can be difficult to work with because they are derivatives of several different pure hues. Generally, if you are working with reds and want to include a brown or rust in your picture, use one that has red in its root color. If you are working with oranges, then the brown to use would be an orange-brown. Likewise, the rust would be in the same orange range.

You can purposely choose a brown that clashes with the other colors in your picture to add interest or attention. If this is your intent, and it is done with care, you can achieve great results. When unplanned, it can be extremely disappointing to use a brown that is visually distracting because it comes from the wrong root color. The artistic effect can be destroyed. Therefore, know what visual outcome you desire and then select the appropriate brown colors.

Tones

The last of the color scales is created by mixing gray with pure colors. This combination results in tones. Depending upon the amount of gray mixed, tones can be lighter, darker, or the same strength as the pure colors they are derived from. When we talk about an object being toned down, we mean that the color has been grayed. Since gray is contained in all toned hues, it is the most natural neutral partner with these colors.

Tones are often used for their wintery effect. Their mood is soft and subtle. Winter scene colors should come primarily from the tone scale. (See photo 14.) Additionally, tones are essential for attaining visual depth. They are also necessary when you are working toward the illusions of mist, fog, haze, or luminosity. In muted winter landscapes, tones are often used to create luster.

Some tones and their root colors include: beige/yellow, rose/red, slate blue/blue, sage green/yellow-green, and heather/violet, purple, or purplish red.

COLOR EFFECTS

While experimenting with the different scales within your landscape pictures, you will notice that colors can emit additional visual and psychological effects. Colors from the warm side of the color wheel appear to advance. Warm colors also tend to give a feeling of happiness, informality, and activity. Hues from the cool side of the color wheel appear to recede. They can exude a psychological feeling of serenity. Cool colors can also be quite formal in their expression. Whenever possible, enhance your desired mood or visual effects by employing any of these subtle color clues.

VISUAL BALANCE

Be sure that your design has a good visual balance. Varying the color value, or the relative lightness or darkness of a hue, will help attain this balance. A picture that is entirely light has a washed-out look. One that includes all dark colors tends to look dull. Scenes which use all medium-ranged hues can lead to disinterest because the design becomes lost. Generally, color values in a landscape need to be varied so that the viewer can easily distinguish between the different elements within the art.

A dominant color is also needed to achieve visual balance in a landscape. When viewing a scene, our eyes naturally rest on the dominant hue within the picture. Consequently, if there is no dominant color, our eyes continue to search to no avail. As a result, we feel discomfort when no color dominance is present, and therefore find we prefer not to look at the art.

Plan your colors so that this psychological reaction doesn't happen to those who view your landscape pictures. Know what your dominant color will be.

AFTERIMAGES

One more very special color relationship is extremely useful when creating landscapes. Notice that when you look at a color for any length of time, you begin to see another hue around its periphery. The new hue becomes more pronounced when the original color is removed from the area. This color phenomenon is called an afterimage. The afterimage of a color is always rather elusive in your mind's eye.

Every color has its own afterimage. However, an afterimage is never a pure color. Rather, it is a very pale tint derived from the hue's complementary color. For example, the afterimage of a red hue will be a tint from the green color family. The specific green is based upon the actual red used. An orange-red will have a different afterimage than a purplish-red. So the green tint afterimage could be mint green, robin's egg blue, or any number of other light greens, depending on the root color. It is important to determine a color's specific afterimage when attempting to use this natural partnership to its fullest potential.

You can incorporate afterimages within your landscape in many ways. Afterimages placed in key positions can create breathtaking awe. For instance, a glowing mist can be developed by using the afterimage for the misty effect. An afterimage can also be a powerful accent in a scene, bringing vitality to the picture. Accentuating the sun by placing a small amount of its afterimage nearby would be a good example of such an accent.

When a painted color and its afterimage are mixed together, the blend of the two hues is a neutral gray. Likewise, when the two partners are combined in a fabric landscape, grays and toned transitional colors have to be used to make the picture look realistic. For example, a sky would include a color and its afterimage with the total range of gradations between the two colors. (See photo 15.)

A sky with such a combination could be a teal blue and its afterimage, apricot. For a realistic blend, gray and several connecting transitional hues would also have to be incorporated. The colors would move from apricot to grayed apricots, with each step moving farther away from apricot and closer to gray. Eventually the transitional colors would lead into the neutral gray. When going from blue to gray, the colors would begin with the blues, working into grayed blues, and then into blued grays. Finally the neutral connecting gray would be reached. (See Figure 2.)

Figure 2.
Combining a Root Color with its Afterimage

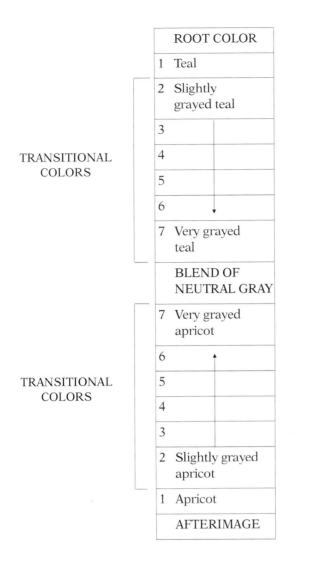

	ROOT COLOR
1	Teal
2	Slightly grayed teal
3	
4	
5	
6	
7	Very grayed teal
	BLEND OF NEUTRAL GRAY
7	Very grayed apricot
6	
5	
4	
3	
2	Slightly grayed apricot
1	Apricot
	AFTERIMAGE

TRANSITIONAL COLORS (upper group, items 2–7)

TRANSITIONAL COLORS (lower group, items 7–2)

To use a color and its afterimage in sky or water, each transitional hue must gradually move toward neutral gray in order to blend with the other color.

Transitional colors are extremely important when working with a color and its afterimage. These colors are not recognized for their beauty; they look drab standing alone. Because of this we seldom buy them, but you should be aware of their existence and their importance in art. Attempt to build your own collection of transitional fabrics, because they are the key to creating fantastic color interactions.

Finding the Afterimage

Using the color phenomenon of an afterimage will enhance your art because it interacts with its natural color partner in a special way. Attempt to use afterimages whenever possible, as they will increase both the beauty and unity within your landscape picture. To discover the afterimage of a particular color, use the following procedure.

Place a white piece of paper on a flat surface under good lighting. Select a color. Cut out a small sample of the color from paper or fabric. (A two-inch square is sufficient.) Put your color sample in the center of the white paper.

Stare at the color sample for at least 15 to 30 seconds, trying not to blink. You may begin to notice a pale color showing faintly on the borders of the sample. It may also dance across the fabric or paper. After you have stared at the sample color for the specified time, carefully take the color away, leaving the white paper untouched. While removing the sample, do not look away from the white paper. Without blinking, continue staring at the paper. In the sample's place a new color, the afterimage, will glow faintly. This afterimage can be very fleeting in its appearance. You may have to repeat the exercise several times to observe it.

If you have trouble finding the afterimage, stare at the color swatch for a longer amount of time, perhaps 30 to 60 seconds. If you wear glasses and have difficulty finding the afterimage, take them off. Repeat the exercise.

Consider using the Letraset Pantone® Color Paper Selector (uncoated) to keep a notation of any selected afterimage hue. While you see the color image before you, quickly flip through the colors to find the one most similar. This may have to be done several times to verify that you have found the correct color.

In summary, creating a work of art that uses color to its best advantage takes forethought. With some experience you will find it both fun and easy. First, you need to design your landscape to incorporate the features that you want to include. After that, you can determine your color choices. Be sure to plan for a visually balanced design with a good variation of color values. Also, use the color scales that best fit your artistic intentions. If it is appropriate to use an afterimage, plan for its inclusion. When you use color to its fullest scope, your landscape picture becomes a lovely work of art.

Chapter II
Visualizing In Color

The best color training we can have is observation and hands-on experience. Color should be an expression of emotion or spirit, not a binding, prescribed formula. Our artistic endeavors should be creatively spontaneous and intuitive in nature—never academic. If you want to increase your color understanding, give yourself permission to take time to look closely at your environment. The greatest guide to color theory is nature. Therefore, let your eyes feast on the sky, water, meadowlands, hillsides, mountains, deserts, grasses, clouds, flowers—the entire world.

Begin to analyze nature's way of using colors. Look at the innumerable greens in vegetation, clashing and blending in unusual ways. Peek at the unexpected colors hiding inside flower centers. Study the variegated colors of roses, rhododendrons, camellias, dahlias, and tulips. Examine different species of trees, observing the color, texture, and design differences of both the bark and the leaves. Notice the changes in the morning and evening skies, and the difference between a winter and a summer day. Scrutinize the subtle designs and colorings of rocks, shells, and sand.

Study the designs and colors of boulders, soil, marble, brick, and tile, realizing that their differences often relate to the location of their origin. Observe the meadowlands with their splendid array of colorful wild flowers, and reflect upon the beauty of the farm lands with their fine color and textural contrasts made by the varied crops being cultivated.

Explore both the obvious and the subtle that nature provides for us. Through observation and analysis, you will acquire a new awareness for the world of nature. Once you begin to make these observations, the surroundings that you live with daily will no longer be taken for granted or looked at superficially. You will find that nature becomes an ever-present companion, offering you new opportunities to observe, to learn, to inspire, and lastly—to create.

Upon close inspection, you will notice that perfect gradations of colors are not needed to create beauty. Even nature doesn't require that. Its use of color is quite unpredictable. Unexpected splashes of color give vitality and freshness to nature. When creating, give yourself license to be equally impulsive with your color choices. Don't feel you must stay within a set color combination of order or predictability. Choose colors from your own personal happenings and from the inspiration that you receive from nature. You will find through your exploration that colors can set a mood, affect your emotions, and help create visual illusions and images.

THE SKY

The mood of a landscape picture is generally dictated by the sky. The actual colors used, the intensity of those colors, and their specific placement within the sky all play an important role in setting this mood. A sky can be as emotive as a poetic song, bringing us drama, excitement, serenity, or reflectiveness. You can create storms, spectacular sunsets, mellow mornings, or even gray days. The sky colors can also reflect the time of day, the season of the year, or the existing weather. By becoming more familiar with various sky conditions, you can create fantastic sky imageries. (See photos 5, 8, 9, 10, 25, and 29.)

If your day begins at sunrise, you know that early morning skies are generally light, airy, and uplifting in feel. The birth of a new day can be created visually by incorporating many tints into the sky area—pinks, peaches, apricots, lavenders, creams, and most particularly, yellows. Also, you can include soft tones such as ecru or beige. If you use pure colors in a sunrise, place them sparingly in your picture; otherwise it may seem unrealistic. Shades would be very unusual in a sunrise, as they are really too dark for early morning colors. (For examples of sunrise skies, see photos 15, 16, and 21.)

Most of us are well aware of the beauty of sunsets, but we rarely take the time to scrutinize these fleeting glimpses of artistic coloration. Sunsets vary immensely from one day to another, or from one minute to another. They can range from a tranquil blush to colors of breathtaking awe. Their hues and visual impact change with the season of the year.

Upon observation, you will notice that the evening sky begins with a prelude of introductory colors which become more pronounced as the sun moves toward the horizon line. Eventually, the hues turn into dynamic bursts of expansive colorations that relate to the preliminary cast.

Winter sunsets are usually very dramatic. They often use intense colorations. Shades, pure hues, and tones mix together in striking contrasts and clashes for a vibrant effect. The colors streak across the sky in bold, unexpected arrangements. A spectacular sky is never predictable in coloration or placement. There are always surprises. These sensational sunsets often incorporate magnificently strong colors, such as violet, deep blue, magenta, orange, red, yellow, and gold. (See photos 17, 35, 37, and 38.)

If you want to create a dramatic sky, use strong, vibrant colors, including any combination of pure hues, shades, and tones. You should have a dominant color for unity, but the secondary and accent colors will provide the real drama. The colors within the sky should change in an unpredictable fashion, both vertically and horizontally. (See photo 41.)

Summer sunsets are generally less dramatic than those of winter. They often feature cream, rose, grayed lavender, grayed apricot, and light blue. These skies are made primarily from the tone and tint color scales. Pure hues randomly placed in limited amounts may also be present. (See photos 23 and 24.)

Tranquil skies can be created by using soft colors throughout the entire sky area. The colors used should be similar in hue and of low intensity. Muted colors will create a restful mood. When strip piecing the sky for this quiet setting, continue the same horizontal strip coloration from one side of the picture to the other. (See photos 6, 13, 14, and 15.)

In landscape design, depth can be accentuated by placing the strongest sky colors visually closest to the viewer. Those strong colors are located at the top of the picture. As the colors move toward the horizon line, the hues become lighter. (See photos 6 and 13.)

CLOUDS

Another way to show depth is by incorporating clouds within the sky area. Besides depth, clouds bring texture and form to the sky. They also add further interest. When deciding whether to include clouds in your picture, remember that they should only be placed in a landscape if they enhance the design. To avoid clutter in your design, make the details of the clouds as simple as possible.

Even though we think of clouds as fluffy and white, rarely are they pure white. Nor are they simply gray. Instead, clouds are made up of subtle colorations influenced by the hues within the sky. (See photos 8, 9, 10 and 29.) Whenever possible, cloud colors should blend into the sky colors. Generally their edges should be gentle and undefined. Most clouds should not look like white cut-outs plopped onto the sky. When observing clouds, notice that the closer the clouds are to you, the more colors you can discern within the formation. As the clouds recede into the distance and drop closer to the horizon line, the colors fade and become grayer.

The clouds you incorporate into your sky should match the mood that you are attempting to create in your design. A sophisticated landscape needs finely designed and subtly colored clouds. A whimsically styled picture can use clouds that are more primitive in design and color.

WATER

Although the sky is the primary element that sets the artistic mood, lakes, rivers, and other bodies of water can give additional emotive feel to a design. The most important influence on water is the sky coloration. Other circumstances that may influence the color of water are the time of day, weather conditions, depth or shallowness of water, and movement of the water. In both reality and artistic expression, water can glisten like dancing gems, dazzling us with splendorous colors of blue, green, teal, lavender, pink, apricot, gold, or violet. (See photos 1, 13, 15, 25, 29, 35, 36, and 37.)

If you want to show shallow water, use a white, a blush white, a light tint, or even a grayed white. These same colors can create a feeling of turbulence. Dark colors in the water are generally interpreted as depth. This deepness does not have to be made with just dark blues. Plum, violet, charcoal, teal, or dark green can also give the feeling of great depth. (See photos 39, 40, and 41.)

LAND

Sky and water are not the only important elements in a landscape. Other geological features also need special consideration when present in the design. Mountain ranges take additional color planning. Likewise, hills and rock formations need thoughtful color execution, too. All land formations can follow a similar pattern of color organization.

Depending on the reference point, mountains, hills, or rocks can be gentle, rolling land masses, or jagged, sawtoothed giants reaching into the sky. Regardless of the land formation, coloration of these features can be as varied as the artist's imagination. (See photos 1, 4, and 30-33.)

Creating Mountain Ranges

Creating majestic mountain ranges in a picture can be a great challenge. Besides considering the shape of the mountains, you need to plan your color arrangement. You can create mountains using any color family. They can be green, blue, mauve, violet, plum, gray, white, brown, tan, pink, apricot, or any other hue. (See photos 4, 11, 12, 21, and 35.)

If you are interested in realism, note that because of the way our eyes perceive distant colors—and because of the atmospheric particles in the air—mountains, hills, and other land formations take on a blue, lavender, or blue-gray cast when viewed from a distance during the day. Also, in the evening, as the sun sets behind the land, only the silhouette of the hills or mountains can be seen. At that time these formations generally appear black, deep blue, or eggplant purple. (See photos 38 and 43.)

The first step in creating mountain ranges within your design is to decide on a color theme. Then separate your mountain fabrics into small color groups that will equal the number of mountain ranges in your picture. The mountain range that is closest to the foreground should have the fabrics from the darkest color group. If you are using prints, this group should also have the largest and most defined patterns. The next mountain range would have the second darkest colors and more subtly designed prints. As you move farther into the background, the mountains become lighter, more grayed in color, and very blurred in detail. Any prints used should be of an undefined pattern. (See photo 17.)

When you construct a mountain, you have three main choices of coloration. Each method gives a slightly different emotional feeling or look. The same considerations apply when creating hills, rock formations, and other land masses.

First, you can place your selected fabrics in a non-organized fashion. This type of random placement gives a very stratified look to the mountains, with lights, mediums, and darks interwoven among themselves. It is the most common way to place fabrics within mountains. (See photos 2, 4, and 41.)

The second alternative is to place the darkest colored fabrics at the bottom of the mountain. As you build the mountains, the colors become lighter. Eventually, at the peaks, the colors are barely visible. This method makes the mountains look very stable, with the mountain base being darkest. The peaks are beautiful with their light tops set against the sky. (See photo 15.)

You can also develop mountains with the lightest colors at the bottom, working upward into the darkest colorations. This color order evokes a more elusive quality. (See photo 16.)

MIST

You may want to create mist between mountain ranges. If so, it can be done by two different methods. The easiest way is to arrange the colors in order from the darkest to the lightest hue. The lightest colors should be toned. When constructing, begin with the lightest tones. As you work upward, the colors should become darker. This particular method is done using only one color family. This effect gives a thick, foggy appearance and also seems quite wintery.

The other procedure for creating mist uses a color and its afterimage. When you have determined those color families, choose the full spectrum of fabrics that will go from the afterimage, through the transitional hues and neutral grays, and on to the second group of transitional hues and the root color. When constructing, begin with the afterimage colors at the bottom of the range and work in a set order. Continue working the fabrics so that the mountain peaks will be created from the darkest colors. With this method of creating mist, the afterimage colors glow between the mountain ranges. It results in a very beautiful effect, because the sun appears to be burning off the mist.

You can create purely imaginary landscapes or you can recreate scenes that have special meaning to you. If you live in a region where the colorations of skies, sunsets, sunrises, clouds, or land masses are unique, you might imitate those distinctive characteristics. Most geographical regions are noted for their own particular colorations. Gray, orange, green, brown, red, purple—every color suggests a different area of our country and other parts of the world. If you want your picture to be realistic, know the geological colorations for the region you are creating, and use them in your design.

In the end, however, you do have license to determine your own color selection within your landscape, regardless of what nature has chosen. So let your imagination challenge itself. Experiment with your own color palette and paint the world from your own unique perspective.

Chapter III
Creating Illusions

When creating landscape pictures, use visual illusions to create images of your own making. Simply by manipulating colors, textures, and prints, you can suggest certain impressions or illusions within your fabric artwork. From these illusions, the viewer can interpret the art through your eyes, rather than through literal realism. The visual illusions most generally used in landscape pictures are visual depth, luminosity, luster, and reflection. Shadows and highlights can also be achieved with careful attention to color selection.

To attain the desired illusions, it is necessary to know the differences between the four color scales. Each color illusion has its own scale requirements. Depending upon the illusion, the desired effect will be achieved by incorporating either pure hues, tints, shades, tones, or a combination of two or more scales in a prescribed manner.

VISUAL DEPTH

Visual depth is the most important illusion to attain in a landscape picture. A scene simply cannot be successful without achieving this perception. Our best guide for learning about depth is nature. Take time to stroll outside and gaze into the distance. When you look closely, you will observe some of nature's guidelines concerning visual depth.

In a landscape, you will notice that the foreground can be created with hues that have no color relationship to the rest of the scene. Although the middle section and background need not have a mutual color relationship with the foreground, they themselves will almost always have a unity of color.

The foreground colors are the most intense. As well, if textures or prints are included, they will have the strongest and clearest definition. The scale of these print fabrics should be of the largest proportion in relationship to the scale throughout the rest of the picture.

Any hills, mountains, or other land formations located in the middle section of a landscape should be made up of colors which are lighter in value and

of lower intensity than the foreground. In addition, the definition of the middle-distant details should be less distinct than those in the foreground. Therefore, the scale of prints used in this area needs to be smaller than the textural patterns placed in the foreground.

As each land formation recedes into the background, it becomes lighter, grayer, and less distinct than the one placed before it. Therefore, your color choices become more toned and blurred as the land masses ebb into the distance. (See Figure 3.)

When creating fabric landscapes, the use of prints should be limited to small-scaled, obscure, or subtle patterns for distant features. The illusion of depth is lost in distant background land formations when the eye can discern clarity, when the coloration is too pronounced, or when tints are used instead of tones.

When you view your own environmental surroundings, you can observe that land masses situated close together have very slight color differences. (See photos 1, 11, and 16.) In contrast, those significantly distant show distinct color changes. (See photos 40, 43, and 44.) When creating your own landscape picture, let the amount of color gradation between the land formations dictate the desired spatial differences perceived by the mind.

If you are unable to observe the phenomenon of depth perception at first hand, look through books and photographs. See how colors lighten and gray as details move farther into the distance. Also notice that texture and pattern become more obscure as your eyes move from the foreground to the background. These simple observations repeat the rules of nature as they appear to your eyes.

LUMINOSITY

Luminosity, the second visual illusion, can create drama and inspire awe in landscape pictures. It is a very popular effect. Luminous objects are those in which light is generated from within. Examples of luminosity are the sun, a lit candle, a light bulb,

Figure 3. Using Visual Illusions in Landscapes: Depth, Luminosity, and Luster

A. For visual depth, as each land formation recedes into the background, it becomes lighter, grayer, and less distinct than the one placed before it.

B. Luminous elements, such as the sun, are created by following certain guidelines, including the use of colors which are more free of gray than adjacent hues.

C. Luster, or reflected light, is created primarily by using closely gradated colors.

and the moon. In reality, moonlight does not glow itself, but rather is reflected light from the sun. However, when we observe the moon from our viewpoint, it appears to glow. Thus, we think of the moon as being luminous.

When creating luminosity, the background of the picture should be relatively dim or dark. To obtain this effect, there has to be a difference between the value of the glowing object and the background. For example, a glowing candle is more pronounced in a dimly lit room than in full sunlight. The same is true in art. Another requirement for achieving luminosity is that the area which glows needs to be small in size compared to the background. If the luminous area is too large for the background, the effect will be lost.

The most important criterion for obtaining luminosity is the relationship between the colors used for the glowing effect and the hues used in the adjacent area. The background that immediately surrounds the luminous area must be more toned than the glowing section. In other words, the hues encompassing the glowing area must be grayed, and the actual luminous object must either be free from gray or have less gray in its coloration than the adjacent color section. The luminous object can be made from colors of varying values. Light, medium, or dark colors can all appear luminous. Likewise, the surrounding colors can be equally varied.

Remember, the major requirement is that the luminous element be made from colors that are more intense or are more free of gray than the adjacent colors. The adjacent area surrounding the luminous object is not made from color gradations. Instead, luminosity is obtained by having many different toned colors randomly placed next to an area of higher intensity. (See Figure 3 and photos 19 and 21.)

LUSTER

The third visual illusion, luster, sometimes is confused with luminosity. These two illusions at times seem nearly the same, but they actually have important differences. Lustrous objects do not radiate light from within as luminous entities do. Rather, a light from another source shines onto the object, giving it a sheen. Light falling on snow or reflecting onto a pond are examples of luster. A car shows luster when light shines on its metal. A Christmas tree ball is lustrous when a tree light shines on it. A table that has been highly waxed may show luster. Luster can be a soft reflected light, or it can be very vibrant in its reflective quality. (See Figure 3 and photo 24.)

A painter can create a lustrous quality with her palette of paints; you can produce the same effect artistically with fabrics. As with luminosity, when creating luster the background should appear dim, dark, or in the shadows. However, the background

Figure 4. Reflections

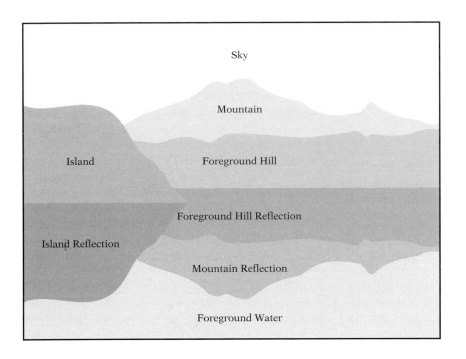

Reflections should appear vertically below the area reflected. The reflection should be equal in height to the object being reflected. Often, daytime reflections are lighter than the object reflected, while night reflections are darker.

for the lustrous effect is generally made of shades. Again, it is important that the lustrous object should be small in area compared to the rest of the field.

Luster is usually achieved by using fabrics which move carefully from the pure color through a gradation of the hue's shade scale. This gradation can incorporate just the lightest shades of the hue, or it can span through to the very deepest values. For best results, use as many color steps as possible when working through your gradations.

When creating a dramatic scene, often a gradation of tints, the pure color, and shades are used. The tints are placed at the point of highest gloss. Then the pure color and shades are added gradually until the darkest hue desired has been incorporated. A color span of this breadth will accentuate the glossiness of the reflection. The glossiest area is achieved from the highest valued colors.

For snow scenes or other lightly colored or toned landscapes, tints and tones may be needed to obtain the desired illusion. Here shades would be too dark to use successfully. When you want to create landscapes such as these, begin the sheen area with a blush white or other high-valued tint. Then move toward the tone scale, keeping your values similar to the other colors within the picture.

REFLECTIONS

Another illusion you may wish to incorporate into your scene is a reflection, or a mirrored image. This can be a beautiful addition to a landscape design. Often a reflection is merely a simple reiteration of the sky colors in a body of water. When you create this illusion, remember that the water colors are usually somewhat lighter than the hues that they reflect. You can also reflect mountains, hills, or manmade structures in the water. (See photos 2, 29, 35, and 38.)

When you incorporate reflections in your landscape design, the points within a reflection should appear vertically below the area reflected. Do not place them at an angle. Also, the reflection should appear to be the same height as the object being reflected. (See Figure 4.) The noted height exceptions are reflections of the moon and sun. With these, the length of the reflection depends entirely on the other design elements in the picture and the visual illusion the artist wants to attain.

Major reflections of mountains, hills, or buildings can be difficult to construct if you attempt to make the reflection before creating the object to be reflected. Therefore, when you decide to create such a reflection in a landscape, consider changing the construction sequence order. Rather than beginning at the bottom of the picture, start at the base of the object to be reflected. From this base, work upward until the entire section of landscape above the reflection line is completed. Then construct the second section of the landscape by beginning with the base of the reflection and working downward to the bottom of the picture. When both sections have been completed, attach them as your design indicates. Through this progression, the illusion of reflection should be very successfully attained in the landscape. (See photo 38.)

SHADOWS & HIGHLIGHTS

Besides these four major visual illusions, you may also decide to incorporate the suggestion of light flowing into your landscape. This can be done by including shadows or highlights. Although both give the suggestion of light, they are quite different in their visual effect and their artistic makeup.

A shadow is visually transparent. Consequently, a shadow never blocks the view of the object it falls upon. Rather, it only changes the color. Thus, when creating the illusion of a shadow, use colors that suggest transparency rather than coverage. To make the shadow look realistic, the edges should be soft and slightly vague.

The shaded area's hue should be one step down on the color wheel from the object's coloration. In addition, the hue should be slightly grayed or shaded. Realistically, a shadow would not be made from a pure color. Thus, a shadow falling on a blue-green object would become a toned or shaded turquoise. Likewise, a shadow resting on an orange land mass would be created from a shaded or toned form of red. (See Figure 1.)

A highlight is quite different from a shadow. It appears opaque rather than transparent. Visually, a highlight seems to cover the object that it falls upon. Highlights are much more intense in color than the actual object being covered.

To obtain the highlight color, use a hue one step higher on the color wheel. In addition, the color needs to be purer in nature than the object highlighted. The exception would be if the highlighted object is already made from a pure color. When this occurs, the highlighted color is simply one step higher on the color wheel.

The highlight of a blue-green article would be a green that is more pure than the root color. The highlight of an orange object would be a form of yellow-orange. It is important to note that a highlight is never lighter than the original color. It is simply more intense and farther up on the color wheel. For that reason, you would never use a tint for a highlight unless you are already working in the tint scale. Doing so would destroy the illusion you were attempting to create.

Illusions can enhance your landscape by giving depth and added interest. Illusions are not difficult to achieve as long as you adhere to their specific requirements. There are many benefits to incorporating visual illusions within your work of art. Most importantly, they will increase the interest and beauty of your landscape picture. You will also feel a great sense of accomplishment if you include any of these illusions in your landscape.

Chapter IV
Making Great Fabric Choices

When making color choices, you are like a painter with her paints, using the array of fabrics that surrounds you as your palette. When creating landscape pictures, your fabrics can be solids, prints, or a combination of both. The decision depends on the picture you want to create, the mood you wish to evoke, the available fabrics, and your personal preference. Patterned fabrics can often enhance the landscape design. At the same time, they can make your fabric decisions much more complex.

When working with print fabrics, you must consider more than color choice. These fabrics can bring interest and texture to your landscape, significantly amplifying the beauty when the selection is excellent. Conversely, many prints are inappropriate for landscapes. Knowing which prints to use for greater beauty and realizing the limitations of others will give you a creative advantage. (See photos 4, 31, and 45.)

Prints are more effective when you practice principles of good fabric selection. When choosing fabrics, attempt to combine a variety of materials that result in harmonious design and color application. The fabrics should form a unified statement. Unless it is your intent, no fabric should stand out conspicuously from the rest. Unintentionally allowing this detracts from your total visual statement.

SCALE
Fabrics work best together when they vary in scale. Whenever possible, try to include a selection of large-scaled, medium-scaled, and small-scaled prints in your landscape. Scale deals with the size relationship a printed pattern has to another. For instance, what may be large-scaled in one group of fabrics may be medium in another, or even small-scaled in yet another collection. When fabrics with the same scale are adjacent, the prints visually bleed into one another. This causes a busy look. Even though most of us have a scale preference, it is best to consciously vary the print scales in our artwork. Doing so generally increases the beauty of our landscape pictures. (See Figure 5.)

With scenic art, fabrics used in the foreground should be the most pronounced in pattern and the largest in scale. As you proceed into the distance, your prints should become more subtle and smaller in scale. Regardless of the general scale used within each design element, it is still important to change the size of print between adjacent fabrics.

A large-scaled pattern can sometimes be used in the background of a landscape if its design is very subtle. This is often achieved by using the reverse side of a fabric. The important factor here is that the design is perceived as purely textural.

VARYING PATTERNS
Along with scale, it is important to vary the subject matter of your print fabrics. Include a variety of floral prints, dots, linear formations, geometric designs, and other interesting patterns. Unless it specifically fits into your focal point, using only one type of print presents a monotonous look. Certainly, you can include several prints of the same theme within an artwork by arranging them throughout the piece. In addition, include several other compatible print designs. Using a variety of designs increases the interest and beauty of your work.

At first glance some fabrics seem totally inappropriate for use in landscapes. However, on closer inspection you may find portions of a fabric which have a textural feel, a specific design feature, or even a definite coloration that you particularly need. Keep your eyes open for fabrics which give the desired impression that you wish to incorporate into your landscape design. (See photos 26, 31, 45, and 46.)

Solid fabrics can be difficult to use when attempting to create the illusion of forests, trees, and underbrush. This applies even more when the designated area encompasses a large portion of the design. The human mind seems to need more definition than solids provide us. Thus, if you are interested in creating landscapes with these features, collect fabrics that have motifs of nature or that show textural lines that could suggest leaf patterns, branches, grasses, fronds,

Figure 5. Varying the Scale and Pattern of Print Fabrics.

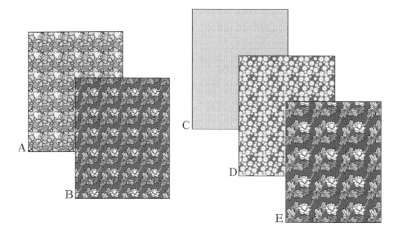

As in prints A and B, using print fabrics of similar scale causes a busy look. These prints visually bleed into each other. Instead, vary the scale relationship between print fabrics, as in C, D, and E. Also vary the subject matter of print fabrics used.

flowers, underbrush, or other such natural vegetation. (See photo 45.)

PROBLEM FABRICS

Even though you have probably acquired many beautiful fabrics throughout the years, you may also have some fabrics in your collection that have obvious design or color problems. There can be appropriate times to use poorly designed fabrics or busy prints, but their use in landscape design is almost nonexistent. Include them only when they fulfill a specific need in the design. Otherwise, stay away from these problem-plagued fabrics, as they will detract from the overall artistic statement that you have worked so hard to create.

Certain prints can cause problems because they do not blend well with other fabrics. Checks, stripes, and large static geometric designs are examples of fabrics which tend to pull out of a design. If you use any of these in your artwork, be aware of their limitations and the possible design complications they may impose on you. For instance, using a checked design in the sky could be disastrous. In contrast, using a stripe for the side of a building may be visually dynamic. Your primary goal is to make all prints work for you. Therefore, include these most difficult fabrics only when they can impart a particular image that you wish to evoke.

Fabrics generally work best when they are made up of one or two color families. The design is created by the variety in the range of color value and intensity, rather than in the number of different colors. This results in a workable, harmonious effect. So for best results, avoid fabrics in which the design includes incongruous color placement. Certainly, exceptions can be made. If you want a busy look, or if a multi-colored fabric is exactly what you need to achieve an illusion, use the fabric. If your landscape picture includes a flower garden, a busy, multi-colored print would not only be acceptable, but might be the best choice.

Like problem prints, stark white fabrics can also be distracting unless used with care. In certain cases, the strength of white can take away from the unity of your artwork by pulling out visually. Before using pure white, ask yourself if an off-white or other neutral might work better. A good substitute for white is often a blush white—a white with just a tinge of color in it. If you are using white without a specific purpose, use it cautiously.

If white allows you to obtain your design objectives, then use it. In scenes which incorporate snow, mountains, clouds, or similar features, limited amounts of pure white can sometimes be used quite successfully. At other times, your preference will be an off-white or blush white.

Selecting the appropriate fabric for your landscape is as important as designing the picture. Prints add an additional element of intrigue. Although prints can often enhance the design, they also complicate the artist's creative decisions. When using patterned fabrics, make your choices carefully and vary the print scale. Stay away from inappropriate, distracting patterns and colorations. Prints are not needed in all landscape pictures, but when you choose to include them, enjoy the process of decision-making.

Always attempt to make the best fabric selection possible for the visual statement you wish to convey. If you feel uncomfortable about a particular fabric, go with your intuition and don't use it in your artwork. As you continue to work toward visual unity within your landscape, you will make great fabric choices.

PART TWO

Procedures

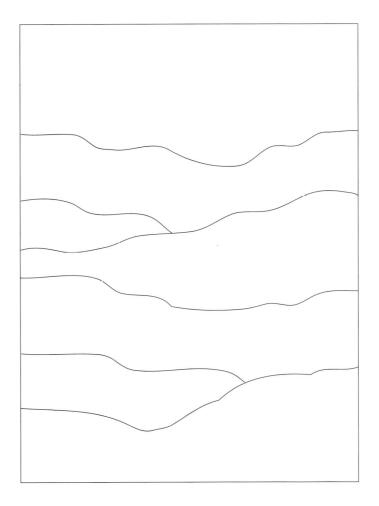

Chapter V
Construction Basics

The technique of stripping, folding, and sewing fabrics to create a landscape can be as simple or as complex as you choose to make it. Before beginning construction, think about the design and colors you wish to use in your landscape. Visualize the picture you plan to create. Let your mind play with the images and the illusions that will be included.

Once you know what you want to incorporate in your picture, make your construction drawing. Placing the drawing on 8½ by 11 inch graph paper works best. You may draw your own design, trace, enlarge or reduce a picture, or use a composite of two or more pictures. After drawing the picture on graph paper, color the different design elements. Then number the elements for color selection. (See Figure 6.)

Next, place the grid lines and segment divisions within the construction drawing. Determine the actual landscape size and mark the measurements on the grid lines. Be sure to mark all four sides of the drawing. For guidelines on drawing your picture, reducing or enlarging a design, marking grid lines, and determining the landscape size, see Chapter VIII. See Part V, Landscape Patterns, for examples of construction drawings.

PREPARATION

Because color is so important, it is wise to have a large selection of fabrics available for your landscape. Color variations, subtle changes, and slightly clashing hues all add to the beauty of this technique. It is not unusual to use thirty to a hundred different fabrics in a medium-size landscape picture. Obtain as many fabrics as you can in the color ranges you need. In some hues you will find many choices, while other colors will be quite limited.

Although you can include silk, velvet, corduroy, satin, and blends in your landscape, it is preferable to use cotton, particularly for your first attempt. Silks and certain synthetic fabrics can have difficulty holding a straight position with long horizontal strips. Therefore, their use is limited.

For most landscape pictures ⅛ to ¼ yard of every fabric should be quite adequate, because you will only use a strip or two from each piece. For large projects, you may need greater quantities.

It is not necessary to wash the fabrics before construction if your landscape picture is intended to hang on a wall. The beautiful sheen of polished cottons is reduced during laundering. The crispness of cottons is sometimes lost in that initial laundering, too. However, if your landscape project will get con-

Figure 6. Design Elements

Each different landscape feature within the picture is a design element. Each element is numbered for color selection. Number the elements in sequential order.

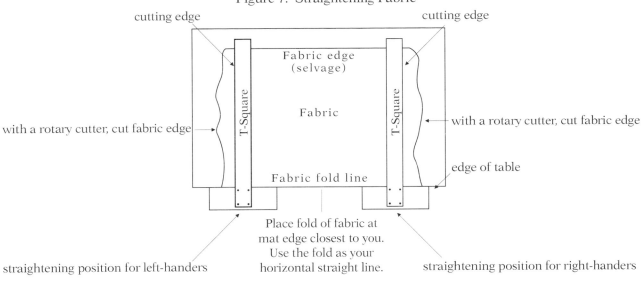

Figure 7. Straightening Fabric

cutting edge   cutting edge

Fabric edge
(selvage)

T-Square   Fabric   T-Square

with a rotary cutter, cut fabric edge   with a rotary cutter, cut fabric edge

edge of table

Fabric fold line

Place fold of fabric at
mat edge closest to you.
Use the fold as your
straightening position for left-handers   horizontal straight line.   straightening position for right-handers

siderable wear or acquire unusual amounts of dirt or dust, wash your fabrics beforehand.

After you have determined which fabrics to include in your landscape, put them in different stacks, with each collection representing a different design element. (See Figure 6.) While construction is in progress, set aside all stacks except the specific ones you are using.

Whenever possible, match the thread to the fabrics in the picture during construction. Because the colors in a landscape continually vary, you will change thread colors several times in the course of the construction. If you do not have matching colors, a neutral gray that is of the same value can be used. Ecru or beige may be used for certain light-colored fabrics.

When there are two different fabric colorations in an area of construction, try to use the identical colors of thread. Put one in the bobbin and the other on the top spool. If this is not possible, choose a neutral hue that will work for one or both fabrics. Do not use black or white thread unless the fabrics are either of those colors. These hues contrast too highly to blend well with non-matching fabrics. From the front side of the picture the stitches may be easily noticed after completion.

Generally, you will work with just a few fabrics at a time—those that are included in the particular strip that you are building. Thus, as you choose a fabric to include in your strip, just press a small portion of the yardage. Your strips will be cut more accurately if the wrinkles have been taken out.

STRAIGHTENING THE FABRIC

After pressing, straighten one edge of the yardage before cutting the strip, using a T square, mat, and rotary cutter. Place one side of the mat on the edge of the table. Fold the fabric in half at its natural fold line. Carefully place the fabric on the mat with the folded side at the table/mat edge and the selvage edge at the top of the mat. Position the T square so that its crossbar is just over the edge of the table. The straight edge of the T square should run perpendicular to the table edge and be set as close to the raw side edge of the fabric as possible. (See Figure 7.)

Once the fabric and T square are in position, place your non-cutting hand on the T square. With your other hand, cut the fabric with a rotary cutter. As you move the rotary cutter along the edge of the T square, keep repositioning your other hand on the T square, so that it continues to be in line with the moving rotary cutter. The weight of your hand will keep the T square stable. Either begin cutting at the selvage edge of the fabric, moving toward yourself, ending at the fold line and the T square crossbar, or begin cutting at the fabric fold line and crossbar and move away from yourself, ending at the selvage edge. Personal preference dictates your direction.

Once you have straightened a particular fabric, you should not have to do so again for any additional strips. However, if you use the fabric later and find that the edge is not perpendicular to its fold line, you will have to restraighten it.

CUTTING FABRIC STRIPS

To cut strips, use the same basic procedure as for fabric straightening. In addition, use metal or plastic strips or a ruler to mark the determined cutting width of each fabric strip. The cutting width of a strip is a

Figure 8. Strip Width

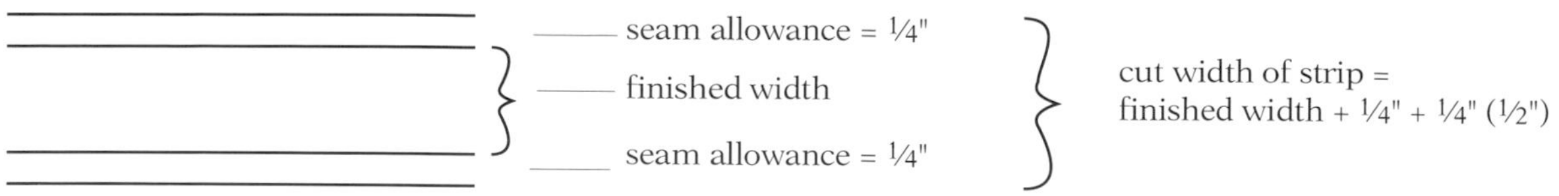

seam allowance = ¼"

finished width

seam allowance = ¼"

cut width of strip =
finished width + ¼" + ¼" (½")

combination of the finished width plus two seam allowances of ¼ inch. (See Figure 8.) Once the cutting width has been noted on the fabric, the T square is placed at the exact cutting position. The fabric is then cut with the rotary cutter.

Although strips can be cut using other methods, a T square gives the most accuracy. Often a slight V will appear at the folded edge of a strip when the cutting has been inaccurate. This V indicates that the strip is not perpendicular to the folded edge or selvage. When this occurs, it can present a construction and hanging problem. Therefore, take the time to recut the strip.

When you cut the first strip of your landscape, make it at least one inch wider than the desired finished width. Do the same for the last strip in the design. This extra width allows for fabric adjustments during the final straightening process of your landscape picture. Any excess fabric can be cut off at that time. For most wall pictures, the majority of the finished strip widths will range from ¼ inch to 1 inch. If a picture is over 30 inches tall, strips up to 1¼ inches can also be used.

In a large piece such as a bed quilt, the finished strip widths can be wider. You would use very few, if any, ¼-inch-wide strips on such a large piece, because they become lost. Depending upon the height of your picture, you can incorporate some strips that are as wide as three to four inches. This would have to be done with care, as colors do not always blend well in such large widths. If the composition of your picture works well with wide strips, then use them. (See photos 39 and 45.)

CONSTRUCTING THE HORIZONTAL STRIPS

The landscape top should be constructed wider than the proposed finished picture. Add at least two inches on each side for this margin. The extra width allows for adjustments during the straightening process. After the first two horizontal strips have been sewn together, place large-headed pins at each end of the bottom strip to mark the actual finished width of the picture. (See Figure 9.)

The landscape design is developed by folding one fabric strip over another while the strips are placed in a horizontal position on the work surface. Each fold marks the specific place where the fabrics change in the design within a horizontal plane on the drawing. The slant of the fold line is determined by the angle to be duplicated from the construction drawing. (For instructions, see Chapter IX.)

When folding one strip onto another, the fabric strip that is visually in the background is the bottom strip. The fabric strip which represents the closest feature in the design is folded onto the first fabric. If there is no difference in visual appearance between the placement of the two strips, then it doesn't matter which fabric is folded onto the other. When positioning, leave both strips at full length until they have been sewn together. This will help you avoid miscalculating the needed length and cutting the fabric strips too short before they are sewn together.

Construction Sequence

Begin constructing your landscape by following the construction drawing, starting at the bottom of the design. Continue working upward until you reach the top of the design. The actual construction of the landscape is worked simultaneously in two separate processes. Thus, during the construction stage, think of your picture in terms of both horizontal and vertical design.

You begin by building the design horizontally, one strip at a time. While creating the horizontal strips, think about the design and anticipate the design elements which dictate fabric changes within a particular strip. These changes take place because the design elements are either beginning, in progress,

Figure 9. Construction Margins

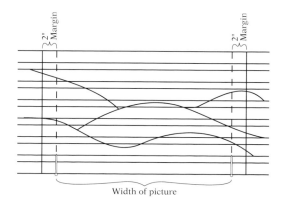

2" Margin

2" Margin

Width of picture

18

Figure 10. Strip Set—a set of strips

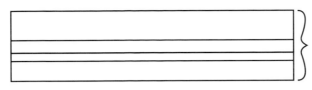

A strip set is a combination of 2 or more strips sewn together vertically.

Figure 11. Segments

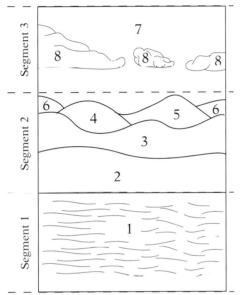

Segments are marked by horizontal dashes in construction drawing. Sometimes they can be along the same horizontal line as a design element or a grid line.

Figure 12. Staystitching

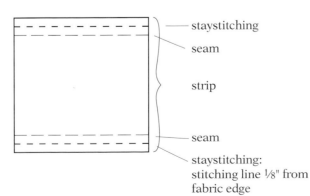

— staystitching

— seam

— strip

— seam

— staystitching: stitching line ⅛" from fabric edge

or ending within your drawing. Concurrently, you need to be aware of the horizontal measurements of both your sewn strips and the construction drawing so that they relate to each other.

In most complex landscape constructions, the majority of time is spent creating the different design elements within the horizontal strips. For each new horizontal strip, you will determine how many different fabrics will be included at that specific place on the construction drawing. Then choose your fabrics from the appropriate stacks.

Determine the order of sewing sequence and the desired finished width of the strips. Then straighten, measure, and cut the selected fabrics. After you have cut these fabrics into strips, sew them together in the order of their placement within the design.

Emotional Impact

When the drawing indicates that only one design element runs across the entire horizontal strip in the landscape, you have two possible choices: You may use just one fabric, or you can opt to use several fabrics of varying colorations within the strip. Your decision depends on the picture and the effect that you wish to create. By keeping the fabric color the same throughout the entire strip, the emotional impact can be soothing, the design simplified, and the details more discernable. Breaking the strip into several colorations may elicit additional interest, abstractness, or a more emotive feel. (For contrast, see photos 40 and 41.)

When horizontal fabric strips are joined together without a design change taking place, sew the two strips together at 45 degree angles rather than 90 degree angles. The seam line seems to blend better at the former angle. (See photos 39 and 40.) There may be exceptions to this practice, however. For instance, with some impressionistic pictures, a 90 degree angle works well. (See the foreground of photo 1.)

BUILDING THE SCENE VERTICALLY

While sewing the horizontal strips together, you are also building the scene vertically. This is done by sewing one completed horizontal strip to another. Be aware of the vertical and horizontal measurements of your fabric landscape at all times. Make sure that each measurement continues to relate to your construction drawing.

Construct in Segments

As you construct vertically, you will work with small groups of strips, or strip sets. (See Figure 10.) These strip sets are sewn together into larger pieces called segments. Strips and strip sets are combined into segments so that the strips are not overhandled, soiled, or stretched during the construction process. Within a landscape picture you may have two to six (or more) segments. To determine segments on your construction drawing, divide your landscape into sections based on the design elements. Segments are not equal in size; the lines of division are placed where you think it will be easiest to separate the picture during construction. Segment divisions are marked on the construction drawing by horizontal dashes during the design process. (See Figure 11.) When you begin each new segment, mark the actual landscape width with pins on the bottom strip, always allowing for at least a two-inch margin on either side.

Eliminate Stretching

Before sewing, pin continuously along the entire length of the two strips. Pinning the strips together securely results in better construction and a nicer looking finished product. Additionally, if you are working on a wide landscape picture, some of the fabric strips can stretch with the weight of the other fabrics. Pinning the strips closely together can diminish or stop this tendency to expand.

If you find that one of your fabric strips, such as a polished cotton, has stretched during the sewing or pressing process, staystitch the unsewn edge immediately before adding the next strip. To staystitch, use a regular seam length and sew just inside the seam line within the seam allowance. (See Figure 12.) Staystitching can also be used to stabilize strips of satin, corduroy, velvet, or other fabrics that tend to fray. To control fraying, try to staystitch before the strip has been sewn to the constructed top.

If a fabric strip has stretched significantly, do not sew additional pieces to that particular strip. Instead, begin a new segment, even if your design doesn't call for it. If you continue adding to fabric that has expanded horizontally, this stretching can cause your entire picture to widen, resulting in a curved effect. This can be an unwelcome result if you are attempting to achieve very straight horizontal lines. However, if you are intrigued by this curving and decide that you want to promote a parabolic effect in your picture, allow the stretching to take place by pinning infrequently or not at all. (See photo 19.)

Alternate Sewing Sides

When you are in the midst of vertical construction, sew the strips together, each time alternating the side where you begin sewing. Because the bobbin stitch is more loosely sewn than the stitch from the top spool, if the strips are always sewn from the same direction, a rippling effect results. By alternating sewing sides, the looser stitches are stabilized by the firm, more secure top stitches in the adjacent seams, thereby eliminating slippage.

It is easy to tell from which end of the strip you last sewed because the threads at the beginning of the seam are usually several inches long. Conversely, when a seam has been completed, the thread is usually cut off close to the material, leaving no tail. Thus, the next seam to be sewn should be started at the end where the threads have been closely cut.

V Pinning Technique

Sewing two horizontal strips together is relatively easy because most design elements in one strip do not have to match the next strip at an exact point. Their placement can vary somewhat. In fact, a slightly offset placement often leads to additional beauty in the landscape.

However, when the design dictates exactness, it is extremely important to be able to place and sew the strips together with precision. These points where the design elements must meet exactly are called reference points. When you need to combine two strips at a reference point, use the V pinning method, which stabilizes the reference point pin. (For detailed instructions on reference points and the V pinning method, see Chapter IX, Exercise IV, pages 57 to 58.)

Sewing Narrow Strips

While you are creating your landscape picture, color will continue to play a vital role. There will be times when you want to work with many color variations within a small vertical space. Likewise, you may want to use vivid or highly contrasting hues in the picture. To obtain these types of beautiful color interactions in a landscape, use very narrow 1/4 inch strips. It is difficult to make perfectly straight 1/4-inch-wide strips using the sewing machine guide in the conventional manner. Thus, when incorporating 1/4 inch finished strips, utilize the 1/4 inch precision sewing method. To do this, position and pin your strips together so that the last seam line sewn is the next strip's sewing guide. (For detailed instructions, see Chapter IX, Exercise VI, page 60.)

Sewing 1/4-inch-wide strips in this manner results in perfectly straight strips on the finished side of the landscape. However, on the back side, the second seam allowance is usually quite uneven. If you were to sew the second seam of a 1/4-inch-wide-strip in the conventional manner, the second seam allowance would be perfect and the finished 1/4-inch-width strip that is seen from the front side would be uneven. Learn this simple technique so that you can create perfectly straight 1/4-inch-wide sewn strips.

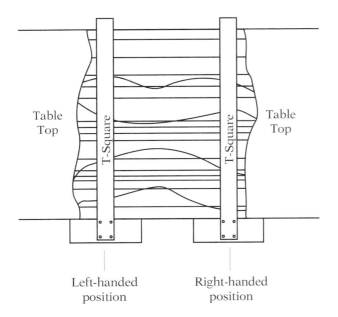

Figure 13.
Preliminary Straightening

Table Top

T-Square

T-Square

Table Top

Left-handed position

Right-handed position

Straighten the first side by placing the landscape right side up on the work table. Position the T square on the landscape as pictured. Mark and cut the first side. Then turn the landscape upside down on the work table. Reposition the T square on the uneven side. Mark and cut.

CONSTRUCTION TIPS

During construction you will want to do some pressing of your work. A dry iron is preferable to a steam iron. If you use the latter, do so with care to avoid stretching your strips. There is no strict rule about how often to press your strip sets during construction. Personal preference is the deciding factor. Work in the manner that seems best suited for your situation.

When ironing, press the finished side first, then go to the backside to straighten the seam allowances. It is your choice whether to press the seam allowances to one side or to press them open. If you press them to one side, the seam allowances should be pressed to the darkest fabric. In some instances where fabric changes take place within strips, you may have to clip the seam allowances at color change points so that fabrics change pressing directions as the dark and light colors change.

When sewing ¼ inch strips during construction, it is best not to press until both edges have been sewn to adjacent strips. If you press before the second seam has been sewn, the seam allowance will get in the way when you sew the next seam.

As you progress through your landscape picture, pin each finished segment on a wall and look at it from a distance. If obvious design or color changes need to be made, do so at this time. If you need to rip out a seam, cut every fourth or fifth stitch with your seam ripper from the side of the bobbin-stitched seam. The bobbin thread is the loosest of the two threads, and thus the easiest to rip. Do not rip seams by cutting threads while pulling the strips apart. This causes stress and holes in the fabric.

After making any needed changes, staystitch around all four sides of the completed segment. You can sew the segments together as you finish them, or you can wait until the entire picture is completed before sewing these sections together.

BORDERS

After construction of your landscape has been completed, you can add borders. Border size and fabric selection should relate closely to the picture. For instance, the border should never be so large that it overwhelms the scene or competes with the focal point. In addition, when choosing border fabrics, use those that have already been included in the picture. Exceptions can be made if new fabrics are added with extreme care. Either way, the addition of a border should result in both visual unity and balance. When used effectively, a border is an accent that enhances the picture.

FINISHING STEPS

Once your landscape has been completed, with or without borders, press the top well on the front side. Then press the backside, making sure the seam allowances are flat and the excess threads are cut. Check for dark threads hiding underneath seam allowances. Also check for dark fabrics pressed on the side of lighter ones. This can show up in the finished scene and can cause distraction. Make a preliminary straightening at this time. (See Figure 13.)

When you have completed your landscape top, you will have finished the most important and difficult stage of the entire project. You will then be ready to begin the next step.

Chapter VI
Basting And Quilting Techniques

Tradition seems to dictate that if you are an American quilter, you will most likely perform one more major step before you consider your landscape picture near completion. You will quilt the scenic top to a middle layered batting and a backing fabric. However, if you are without a quilting background, or if you are a patchworker from another country, it is quite possible that you will skip the basting and quilting process.

In many countries where patchwork is done, the quilting process is not included in a fabric creation. With quilting being neither a tradition nor considered a necessary component in the design, batting (or wadding) is not easily available to many patchworkers throughout the world. When it is obtainable it can be extremely expensive. The choice of whether to quilt your fabric art is an individual matter, and your decision generally reflects both your personal preference and the traditions you are bound to. (For an excellent example of a nonquilted landscape picture, see photo 4.)

Although landscape pictures can be quite stunning without quilting, this extra dimension can give you the opportunity to add further details, texture, and depth to your design. Through quilting lines you can create an image, set a mood, or promote an idea. The quilting lines and constructed top form an interlocking visual partnership within the landscape.

BATTING

The beauty of quilting is somewhat enhanced by the type of batting used. Batting adds density, thus giving additional dimension to the picture. If you hand quilt, use your favorite batting and work in the manner you are accustomed to.

For machine quilting, it is unwise to use 100% polyester batting because it can shift during the quilting process, no matter how well you baste. This shifting can cause distortion so that the picture will not hang flat against a wall. Thus far, the best batting to use for machine quilting is one made from a cotton/polyester blend. A batting such as Fairfield's

Cotton Classic® Blend is an excellent choice for machine quilting.

Cotton blended battings should be preshrunk unless stated otherwise on the package instructions. You can do this by running hot water through the folded batting in a large sink. Then gently squeeze as much water from the batting as possible. Carefully unfold the wet batting and place it into the dryer. Dry at a hot temperature. When dried, the batting will come out of the dryer softer and somewhat smaller in size.

BASTING

Once your top has had its final pressing and your batting is prepared, you are ready to begin basting. Cut the backing material and batting the same size as the top. With masking tape, secure the backing fabric to the table, wrong side up. To do this, line up one edge of the backing fabric with the table edge. Then tape the backing material securely to the table without pulling at the fabric. After the backing is secured, place the batting on top of it.

Next, carefully position the landscape picture onto the backing and unsecured batting. Place the

Figure 14. Basting

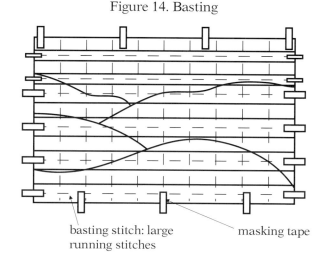

basting stitch: large
running stitches

masking tape

Place masking tape on each side of strip to be stabilized. Baste every taped strip. Baste vertically after horizontal basting has been completed.

bottom edge of your picture at the table edge. Secure the picture to the table by taping at least every 2 inches on each side of selected horizontal strips. If necessary, straighten the strips by pulling them slightly as you tape, being careful not to put undue stress on the horizontal strips. (See Figure 14.)

For vividly colored strips or any strips that have strongly visible horizontal lines, be sure to tape them on both sides of your picture. Because it is important that these particular strips are horizontally straight, you may baste closer than every two inches.

Begin basting horizontally at the bottom of the picture. Thread a long, sharp needle with regular thread. With the needle in your sewing hand and a teaspoon in the other, baste across each horizontal strip that has been taped to the table. The teaspoon is used to lift the needle tip upward through the three layers of cloth each time the needle hits the table top. (See Figure 15.) After you have completely basted the picture horizontally, baste vertically about every two inches. When finished, carefully untape the landscape from the table.

Now you are ready to quilt by hand or machine. Which method you use is purely an individual decision. Both hand and machine quilting can give wonderful visual effects when well done.

HAND QUILTING SUGGESTIONS

One of the advantages of quilting by hand is that you have more control over your stitches than you have with a sewing machine. The stitch length can also be made much smaller than those done on a machine, although consistent size can be a concern. The one major disadvantage to hand quilting is the time involved.

For hand quilting a strip pieced landscape, a betweens/quilting needle, size 9, works best. Smaller needles tend to break easily when going through the seam allowances. Larger needles make it more difficult to keep your stitches small.

If you use a quilting hoop, baste a four-inch-wide extension on all sides of your landscape. This allows you to quilt into the sides and corners of your picture with ease. When the quilting is completed, take the extensions off.

For hand quilting, I prefer a fourteen-inch hoop, even when working on a large bed quilt. This size allows me to quilt effortlessly within the hoop while keeping my body and arm in a comfortable position. The one disadvantage to this small hoop is that it has to be repositioned often.

Figure 15.
Spoon Basting

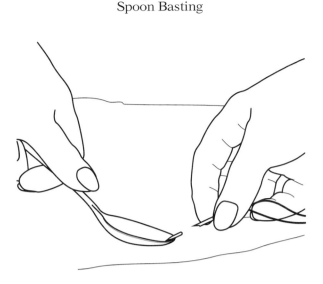

When hand quilting, I prefer to use the highest quality sewing thread available rather than quilting thread. Unlike most quilters, I change the color of my thread each time my quilting moves to a new fabric color. It takes longer to quilt in this manner, but the results are worth it. The result is that the viewer is only aware of the texture and the detail of the quilted line—the actual quilting stitch is not noticeable. (See photos 17, 18, 19 and 20.)

Many people who use this method begin by threading several needles, each with a different color. Then, when they come to a fabric color change, they just pick up the needle with the matching thread. This generally works better than using just one needle for quilting, as you don't have to rethread as often.

When hand quilting, thread your needle while the thread is still attached to the spool. If you cut first, you may inadvertently put the wrong end of the thread through the needle. When this happens, as you sew or quilt you pull the thread in the opposite direction from which it was constructed. In other words, you force the thread to go against its grain while sewing. This causes the thread to break down quickly, often resulting in twisting, knotting, and fiber separation, which can make hand sewing or quilting a difficult task.

MACHINE QUILTING SUGGESTIONS

Machine quilting your landscape picture will give you two main advantages. The time it takes to quilt your piece will be very short compared to hand quilting. Also, machine quilting lends itself to techniques which produce frequent multiple layers of fabric to quilt through. Disadvantages may include the fact that some sewing machines show little tolerance for the quilting process. It can also be difficult to control the machine so that it sews the quilting stitch exactly as you want. Also, large pieces present a problem with their bulk. As in hand quilting, excellent machine results take practice.

Thread type and color are factors to consider if you decide to machine quilt. When colored thread is used, the quilting stitches are very visible. For some people these stitches are distracting. If you want the thread to be less noticeable, so that the viewer is merely aware of the texture and design developed by the quilting stitches, use clear nylon thread. (Use a dark clear nylon thread for very dark fabrics.) You can find nylon thread at almost all fabric stores, as well as in many quilt shops.

Because nylon thread is very fine, use an equally fine needle for your machine quilting. A regular sewing machine needle leaves noticeable holes in the fabric because the needle is wider in diameter than the nylon thread. These holes can be distracting to the viewer. Consider using a universal size 60/8 or 70/10 (European/American) or other fine needle. These needles break easily from the stress of quilting, so keep a package of replacements on hand.

When machine quilting, I prefer to use nylon thread in both the bobbin and the top spool. Contrary to reports warning against this, machine quilting in this manner has not harmed my machine. I have found that a sewing machine works best when identical thread is used in both the bobbin and the top spool, regardless of the type of thread. Tension problems often arise when different threads are used, even when the differences seem slight.

If your machine will not handle nylon thread, assess your alternatives. Using a regular thread in the bobbin or regular thread for both may be options. If you decide to use nylon thread in your bobbin, take care when putting it onto the bobbin. Do not wind it quickly, as the thread may stretch in the process.

Machine Preparation

Every machine is different, so experiment with your own machine to see what adjustments are needed for quilting. Try to do only those that seem absolutely necessary. For machine quilting, it is not necessary for me to change the tension of my machine, nor do I put the feed dogs down. I simply change needles, adjust the stitch length, and replace the presser foot with a quilting foot. A walking foot or quilting foot is extremely helpful to attain beautiful machine quilting; it makes it easier to control the stitching. You can buy a special quilting foot from a sewing machine dealer.

The last preparation before quilting is to clean and oil your machine. Open the bottom section and clean out the dust and fluff that has built up from piecing. Be sure to clean around the bobbin casing. While doing this, oil your machine if necessary. Insert a new needle for quilting and be sure the needle is the appropriate size for the type of thread you are using.

While machine quilting, dust and fiber particles find their way into the lower part of the machine. If you haven't cleaned prior to quilting, this residue simply adds to the established buildup. This can overwork your machine. It can also cause inferior stitching if left unattended. Make this cleaning a pre-quilting ritual. In addition, dust the sewing table and the outside of the machine thoroughly. Bulky fabric can touch unusual areas of the sewing machine that may have accumulated dirt, oil, or dust. The surrounding area must be spotless to minimize staining or soiling the artwork. When all is in order, it is time to quilt.

Before beginning to quilt, test and adjust the stitch length with scrap materials and batting. Try to use as small a stitch length as possible. As you begin and end each quilting line, you will backstitch three to four stitches, then cut the thread tails as close to the fabric as possible.

QUILTING SEQUENCE

Before quilting, mark the design lines on the landscape top. When hand quilting, you can either mark all of your quilting lines initially or do them as you go. Use your favorite tool for marking: fine pencil, marking pen, chalk, etc. For machine quilting, it is best to mark the quilting lines with something that is easy to erase. If you use chalk, mark only one design element at a time, since it disappears so quickly. When you become more adept with machine quilting, you may quilt without any markings, working spontaneously on the machine.

Begin by quilting the land formation next to the sky. First, outline quilt around the land formation, making the stitching line about 1/16 inch from the outside edge. (See Figure 16.) Then quilt the desired details within that design element. Continue to work downward, marking and quilting each new design element. The last land element to be marked and quilted will be the foreground. After the foreground has been quilted, begin marking and quilting the sky, starting with the areas closest to the background and moving outward to the upper edges of the picture.

ENHANCING
THE SCENIC DESIGN

The quilting lines in a landscape should reflect the lines of nature. Grids and other traditional quilting lines do not work well in scenes, as they tend to confuse the illusions that the artist has worked so hard to attain. Included below are generalizations and observations concerning the use of quilting lines to accentuate the basic scenic design.

Sky Moods

If you have used intense colors in your sky, you can increase the intensity by quilting close together in that designated area. These lines can be further intensified by making them angular in shape. (See photo 38.)

Serenity can be shown by broad, gradually sweeping quilting lines. The quilting should be placed widely apart. (See photos 6 and 13.) If you are moving from an area of intensity to one of calmness, gradually change the quilting lines as you move out of the first area and into the next, making them less sharp in angle and farther apart.

Water Movement

If you have included a body of water in your picture, look at the water currents and wave actions in several photographs. Notice that the water movements are more discernable closest to the foreground. Therefore, quilting lines should be placed farther apart there. As the water recedes into the background, the waves and current become less pronounced. Thus, the quilting becomes closer together until it is almost indistinguishable in the farthest distance. (See photos 1, 15, 25-27, 38, and 39.)

Water movement does not always flow in the same direction throughout a body of water. Changes can be caused by tides, rapid water movement within a narrow channel, or even weather conditions. Do not be afraid to change the water direction in your artwork. Variations add interest. (See photo 41.)

Imitating Nature

Mountain details are easy and fun to create in landscape pictures. Valleys, crevasses, crags, and ice fields can be developed by the placement of quilting lines. Most quilting lines can be placed randomly on the mountain ranges. However, if you have created a picture of a specific mountain that has recognizable crevasse lines, you should use photographs to guide your quilting line placement. (See photo 21.)

If you have designed a picture with mist, be sure not to quilt in the misty areas. In reality, we simply do not see distinctive lines within mist. Therefore, if

Figure 16.
Quilting Line Placement and Sewing Sequence

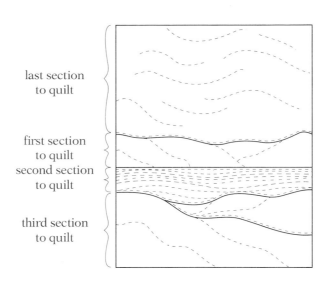

you did quilt in this area, it would destroy the illusion that you have tried to create. (See photo 16.)

With other land formations, observe nature for quilting ideas. For hills you may simply quilt lines which repeat their curving configurations. (See photo 5.) Or, if you want to give the illusion of trees, you can quilt tree formations throughout the hill areas. Strata composition is very important when creating rock formations and dry land areas. If you have used fabrics that bring out this illusion, it will be much easier to quilt by following those suggestive patterns. Otherwise, look at books and magazines which include this type of scenery. Note how the configurations of these land masses form beautiful designs. (See photos 31, 32, and 33.)

If you have used print fabrics to give the illusion of vegetation or flowers, consider quilting by following the design lines within the fabrics. Otherwise, study flower, tree, and bush illustrations in garden books, then make your own quilting lines based on your observations. (See photos 9, 45, and 46.)

When you have finished quilting, pull out the basting threads and cut all excess threads. Shake the landscape gently, allowing it to loosen up. Then hang it on a wall. Observe the scene from a distance. Are there any places which need additional quilting? If so, add them.

When you are satisfied with the effect of your quilting, it is time to stop. Do not over-quilt. When quilting is completed, your landscape is ready to be straightened accurately before adding the binding.

A Photo Gallery
of Landscapes

The design of a landscape picture is merely a foundation. It is the way the artist uniquely uses colors and fabrics that gives the scene its individual personality. The artist not only composes a story through visual images, she or he creates a statement of personal style.

This photo gallery is a blending of landscape pictures created by artists who have been inspired by either their own environmental surroundings or special places in their minds. The themes vary, the colors change, but the one important common bond they share is that all landscapes have been created by using strips of fabric to form their images.

Almost all scenes shown are designed and constructed in the manner described in this book. There are a few created by other methods, however. Different methodologies are included to illustrate an important creative truth: To suggest that there is only one way to accomplish a task is to limit countless possibilities and opportunities. In reality, when our collective minds are challenged, we can find many approaches to working through the same technical dilemmas. As your skills increase, permit yourself to explore innovative construction techniques which will further lead to the creation of beautiful scenic images.

1. **View From My Childhood Garden.**
   Joen Wolfrom, 1989.
An impressionistic view of Puget Sound and
the Olympic Mountains. Foreground fabrics
were cut and placed in an intuitive fashion
within each garden strip to create the rhodo-
dendron and azalea blossoms. Owner: Ulster
Folk & Transport Museum, Northern Ireland.
(*Photo: Ken Wagner*)

2. **Where The Wild Rhodies Grow.**
Pat Magaret, Pullman, WA

An excellent example of how strip piecing, appliqué, and patchwork can be combined to make a harmonious statement. Created to commemorate Washington State's 100th birthday in 1989. Shows Mt. Rainier with appliquéd rhododendrons, the Washington State flower. An example of incorporating reflections in a design. (*Photo: Jerry DeFelice; Courtesy of* Quilter's Newsletter Magazine)

3. **Return To Prairie Skies.**
Pat Magaret, Pullman, WA

"I incorporate symbolism that gives special meaning to those for whom the quilts are made. Nature and its constantly changing hues influence all my work. I enjoy experimenting with unusual color combinations." (*Photo: Courtesy of P. Magaret*)

4

5

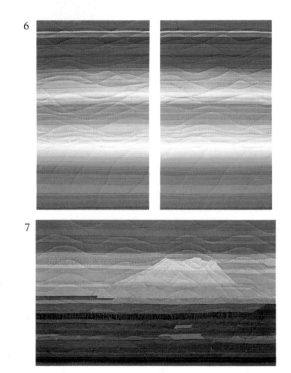

6

7

4. **A Touch Of Spring.**
   Geraldine Gahan, Dunlavin, Ireland.
Fabrics used include 100% cottons, cotton blends, pure silks, and light wools. A wonderful example of using prints to attain images. Very effective textural feeling. An excellent example of fabric art which has not been quilted. (*Photo: Walter Pfeiffer Studios, Dublin, Ireland*)

5. **Pieceful Palouse.**
   Shirley Perryman, Pullman, WA
An excellent example of using color to achieve depth. Solids, prints, and hand-dyed fabrics combine to make this farm land realistic. Toned fabrics work to give an allusive quality to background. (*Photo: Courtesy of S. Perryman*)

6. **Country Evening.**
   Joen Wolfrom, 1985.
An illusion of green grass and evening sky. Quilting lines further the illusion. Cool colors help give a calming effect. Private Owner. (*Photo: Ken Wagner*)

7. **Mount Rainier, My View.**
   Diane Armstrong, Graham, WA
Uncomplicated color and design combine to create a calming work of art. (*Photo: Ken Wagner*)

8

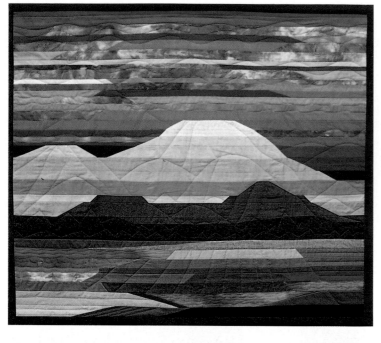

9

10

11

8. **Valley Vision.**
Marion Marias, Fresno, CA
Hand-dyed fabrics and texture add interest to the design. Clouds are subtly formed through color changes within the strips. (*Photo courtesy of M. Marias*)

9. **Garden View.**
Joen Wolfrom, 1989.
An example of using strips of fabric to make cloud formations in the sky. Also, perspective quilting lines in garden accentuate depth. (*Photo: Ken Wagner*)

10. **Looking West**.
Joanne Myers, Bend, OR.
An excellent example of creating beauty and interest in the evening sky. Illustrates how clouds can be formulated through changing colors within a sky. (*Photo courtesy of J. Myers*)

11. **Mountains.**
Judy Sacha, Steilacoom, WA
With a background in watercolor painting, Judy works her designs on paper, first making a half dozen variations. Excellent example of mountain peak construction. Also a beautiful blend of warm and cool colors within a picture. (*Photo: M. Sacha*)

12. **Three Sisters.**
Marie Terhune, Bend, OR.
Landscape is created by vertical construction. Winter effect results from toned colors. The angled jaggedness within the design causes a feeling of excitement and jarring movement. (*Photo courtesy of M. Terhune*)

13. **Sea Breeze.**
Joen Wolfrom, 1985.
A simple exercise in color study. Light reflects from quilting to give additional depth. Flowing quilting lines give feeling of tranquillity. Owners: Dr. and Mrs. K. Schoenfelder. (*Photo: Ken Wagner*)

14. **Evening Repose.**
Joen Wolfrom, 1986.
Exudes a feeling of serenity because colors are closely related cool-hued strips. Introduction of sky colors in the foreground brings unity to the landscape. As land recedes into the distance, the colors lighten and become grayer. Private owner. (*Photo: Ken Wagner*)

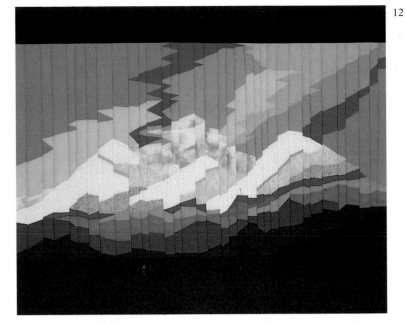

12

14

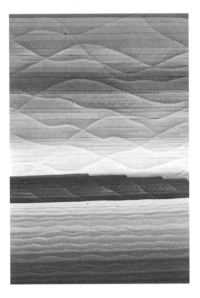

13

15

16

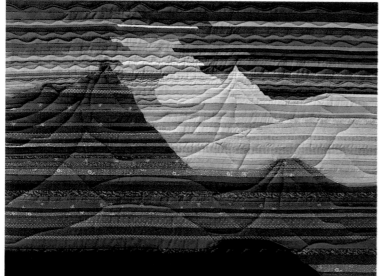

17

15. **Serenity At Dawn.**
Joen Wolfrom, 1985.
A tranquil effect caused by combining a root color and its afterimage, giving a reflection in the water. The calming mood is accentuated by the sky and water colors moving across the entire picture. Owner: Erkki Kauppinen, Finland. (*Photo: Ken Wagner*)

16. **Misty Mountains.**
Joen Wolfrom, 1986.
Mist between mountain ranges. Quilting lines do not continue through areas of mist. Owner: Lingo, Inc. (*Photo: Ken Wagner*)

17. **Setting Sun.**
Joen Wolfrom, 1983.
Reversed fabrics are used for some background effects. Quilting adds extra texture and color changes. Hand Quilted. Owners: Frank and Karen Jung. (*Photo: Ken Wagner*)

18. **Setting Sun.**
Close up of hand quilting detail on textile art pictured in photo 17. Quilting stitches vary in color as thread colors change when moving from one fabric hue to another. Each design element is outline quilted just outside of its formation. (*Photo: Ken Wagner*)

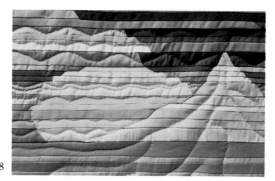

18

19. **Let Freedom Glow**.
Joen Wolfrom, 1985.
A tribute to the birthday of the Statue of Liberty. Curved strips cause a parabolic effect, giving the feeling of a rounded world. Luminosity from the flame is created by using varying degrees of toned fabrics. Owner: The Russell Company. (*Photo: Ken Wagner*)

20. **Let Freedom Glow**.
Close up of detail on quilt pictured in photo 19. Statue of Liberty was made by using strips of innumerable black fabrics. An example of hand quilting with the threads changing colors as the quilting lines move through the different fabric hues. (*Photo: Ken Wagner*)

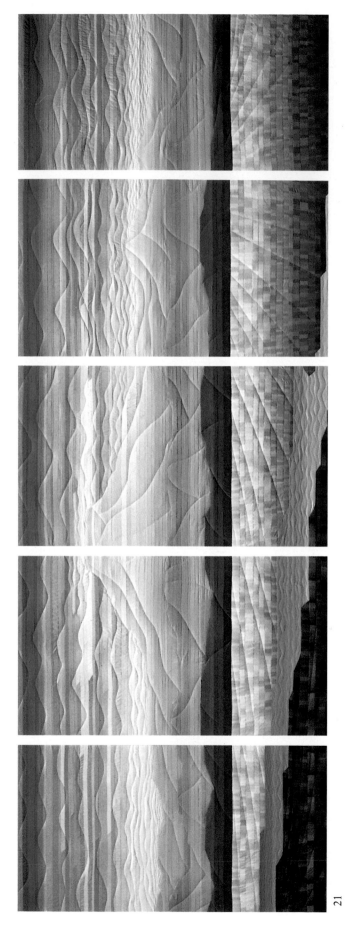

21

21. Springtime In The Valley.
Joen Wolfrom, 1986.

Tribute to Mt. Rainier and the Puyallup Valley bulb fields. Seminole fabric was created for bulb fields. Luminous sunrise effect attained by using yellows that were more pure than the surrounding toned colors. Flowers seem to reflect the light from the sky. Perspective lines accentuate the rows of flowers in the bulb fields. Owner: Summer Hill Retirement Community. *(Photo: Ken Wagner)*

22. Springtime In The Valley.

Close up of the detail from the textile art shown in photo 21. An example of Seminole piecing. Also, machine quilting lines are shown. *(Photo: Ken Wagner)*

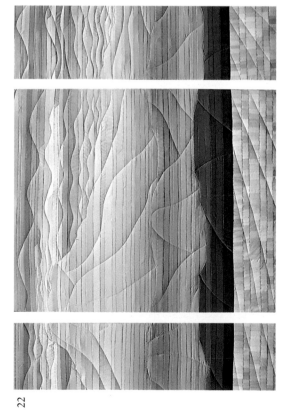

22

24

23. Summer Serenade.
Joen Wolfrom, 1985.
An example of how the partnership between a color and its afterimage can work to give a feeling of quiet unity. Owner: Beuret Investments. *(Photo: Ken Wagner)*

24. Shimmering Sun.
Joen Wolfrom, 1986.
Shimmering sun on the water was made by using Seminole-type fabric. An example of the sun's luster on water. Because of the relatively high color values in this picture, tones were used for this illusion rather than shades. Owner: Diane Perkins. *(Photo: Ken Wagner)*

23

35

25

26

27

25. **Harbor Light.**
Jean V. Johnson, Olathe, Kansas.
All work on this page by Jean was developed in her own style using her own technical methods for creating lovely scenes. Much of her work is inspired by impressions of places that she knows and loves. Pictured here is a Baltimore Clipper Ship on the Chesapeake Bay. Dramatic impact was created by her color choices. Breathtaking sky is alive with coloration. An excellent example of reflection and lightening of colors near the horizon line. Owner: St. Barnabas Medical Center. (*Photo: Courtesy J. Johnson*)

26. **Tidewater—-The Marsh.**
Jean V. Johnson.
Scene indicative of the quiet sanctuaries of the eastern shores of Maryland and Virginia. Excellent choice of fabric for rocks, resulting in textural effect. The quilting also accentuates the texture. (*Photo: Courtesy of J. Johnson*)

27. **Ebb Tide**
Jean V. Johnson.
An example of the beaches along the Atlantic Coast. Shows the beautiful blend of a root color and its afterimage within a design. Transitional colors are toned. The total effect is one of subtle harmony. (*Photo: Stephen Attig*)

28

28. Canadian Suite.
Ann Bird, Ottawa, Ontario, Canada.
An abstract vision of the aurora borealis in a vertically stripped construction. Owner: Miriam Simpson. (*Photo courtesy of A. Bird*)

29. Pearson Charm.
Ann Bird, Ottawa, Ontario, Canada.
An impressionistic Vancouver Island scene created by cutting charm quilt blocks into strips and resewing them into a scene. Example of using reflections in the design. Owner: The White Museum of the Canadian Rockies, Banff, Canada. (*Photo: Courtesy of A. Bird*)

30. Andes Mountains.
Lorraine Doyle, Victoria, British Columbia, Canada.
Excellent example of visual depth. The sky colors enhance the design by contrasting with the mountains. Good fabric use for intriguing textural changes. (*Photo: Courtesy L. Doyle*)

31. For Ansel.
Karen Wooten, Poway, California.
"A vast and growing collection of black and white fabrics and a fascination with the strong contrasts that mark the work of Ansel Adams inspired this piece." Textures and prints are used to emphasize the design. (*Photo: Ken Wagner*)

29

30

31

33

34

35

32. **Desert Reflecting.**
Carol B. Wheeler, Hayden Lake, Idaho.
Inspired by a R.C. Gorman lithograph. There are over 140 different fabrics in this design. A combination of strip piecing and hand appliqué. (*Photo: Courtesy of C. Wheeler.*)

33. **Abraham 4:9.**
Carol Johnson, Nibley, Utah.
Picture was designed from a photograph of the Colorado River in the Grand Canyon. Strata effect of canyon walls is accentuated by the slanting strips. (*Photo: Courtesy of C. Johnson*)

34. **Sunset Solitude.**
Phyllis Danielson, Sarasota, Florida.
"Most of my inspirations come from nature..." A soft, subtle mood evoked by color choices. (*Photo: Courtesy of P. Danielson*)

35. **Winter Sunset**.
Joen Wolfrom, 1986.
Darkest sky colors near horizon give different feeling than sky colors in photo #15. Example of sky reflection in water. Owner: Nancy Mork. (*Photo: Ken Wagner*)

36

37

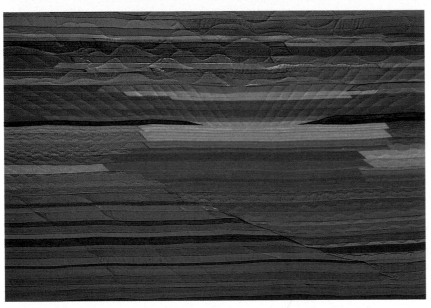

38

36. **Shasta Lake.**
Marie Terhune, Bend, Oregon.
An example of a beautiful blend of color and afterimage hues. (*Photo: Courtesy of M. Terhune*)

37. **Evensong.**
Signe Twardowski, Tacoma, WA.
An abstract landscape showing water and sky with a dramatic sunset. Quilting lines play an important role in the definition of design. (*Photo: Ken Wagner*)

38. **Night Glow.**
Joen Wolfrom, 1984.
A study of mountains silhouetted in the evening sky while reflected in the water below. Large variety of black fabrics were used. Quilting lines show the intensity of the sun by being placed close together at the most vibrant coloration and by their angular formation. As emotion lessens with color, the quilting lines become less intense by decreasing their angular forms and by being placed farther apart. Private owner. (*Photo: Ken Wagner*)

39. **The Mountain Is Out.**
Joen Wolfrom, 1985
Water colors change hues to show depth. Water colors include blue, green, teal, pink, blush white, periwinkle, and gray. Foreground fabrics introduce sky colors. Narrow strips of water colors were combined with wide strips of land. Owner: Gretchen Wilbert. (*Photo: Ken Wagner*)

40. **Moonlight Sonata.**
Joen Wolfrom, 1985.
Using narrow strips of nearly clashing colors makes a beautiful display of color interaction which imitates the unpredictability of nature. To add calmness to the design, strip colorations continue from one side of the picture to the other in the sky. Owner: Don Kelley. (*Photo: Ken Wagner*)

41. **Evening Tranquillity.**
Joen Wolfrom, 1985.
An emotive, abstract style achieved by random changing of the sky colors, both vertically and horizontally. Using narrow strips allows for more color movement. White in water gives the feeling of turbulence. Quilting lines change direction in the water. Owner: Morford's, Inc. (*Photo: Ken Wagner*)

40

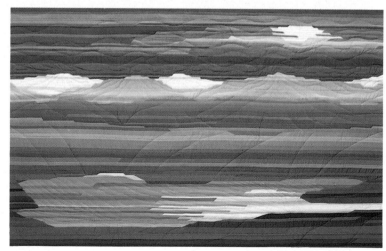

41

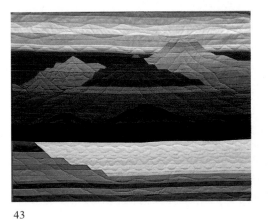

42. **Moonlight Over Mt. Edgecumbe.**
Janine Holzman, Sitka, Alaska
Unpredictable stars add interest to the design. Artist used her unique environmental surroundings to create a special scene. Good example of using shades to express an evening scene. Owner: Robert Scavron. (*Photo: Ken Wagner*)

43. **September Mountain.**
Martie Huston, Santee, California.
Scene illustrates good visual depth. Water colors seem to glow from the sky reflection. (*Photo: Ken Wagner*)

44. **Sunset.**
Sally Kimmell Glutting, Sandpoint, Idaho.
Her inspiration was first taken from a photo in a book, then from the beautiful sunsets in northwestern Montana. (*Photo courtesy of S. Glutting*)

42

43

44

45. **Beyond The Forest.**
Joen Wolfrom, 1989.
Vertically constructed. Prints were used to accentuate the forest underbrush. Almost all print fabrics were reversed. Luminous effect of the sunlight was created by using colors that were less toned than the surrounding fabrics. Scene was developed intuitively, rather than from a drawing. (*Photo: Ken Wagner*)

46. **Awakening.**
Erika Carter, Bellevue, Washington.
Vertical strip pieced technique using fabrics in a very individualistic style. Use of shades gives an autumnal feeling. Owner: Gayle Bean. (*Photo: Ken Wagner*)

Chapter VII
Straightening And Finishing Techniques

Unlike a block-designed quilt that uses its modules to determine the physical outside boundary, strip pieced landscapes require other methods to straighten their sides. These artworks are difficult to straighten because the only reference points are horizontal lines which cannot be relied on for accuracy. To complicate matters, there are no precise vertical references, so the perpendicular sides cannot be established by conventional methods. Thus, the entire straightening process can be difficult.

After attempting several different methods, I believe that the most accurate way to straighten a strip pieced landscape is by a plumb line straightening technique. This approach, which has evolved through much experimentation, works well for all sizes and types of fabric art that do not have a natural visual boundary line. To begin, set aside large-headed pins, topstitching thread (or other thick thread), a yardstick or meter stick, scissors, chalk or other marking tool, and a T square. Study Figure 17.

FINDING THE HORIZONTAL PLUMB LINE

Place your landscape picture on the table or floor. Then pick out the horizontal strip that has the strongest visual impact. This strip is the one that you are most drawn to because of its color strength or its placement in the design. Place a large-headed straight pin on either end of this strip. Both of the pins should be positioned exactly at the lower seam line of the strip, with the pin points facing toward the center of the landscape. This horizontal strip can be located anywhere in your picture.

Take the topstitching thread and wrap it around one of the pins with a figure-8 pinning. To do this, attach the thread by wrapping it around a large-headed pin, alternating from pin head to pin point in a figure-8 manner. (See Figure 18.) After the thread has been secured with that pin, take the attached thread to the opposite pin. Wrap it around the second pin in figure-8 fashion. The thread should be taut. Cut the thread away from the spool. You have just made the horizontal plumb line.

MARKING THE UPPER HORIZONTAL PLUMB LINE

Your next step is to mark the upper horizontal plumb line. This line determines the landscape's top edge. Establish the exact distance between the horizontal plumb line and the selected top edge of your quilt. Place a pin on either side of the quilt with the pin points facing horizontally inward. Both pins must be an equal distance from the horizontal plumb line. As before, wrap the thread around the two pins in a figure-8 fashion. Cut the thread from the spool. The thread line should be straight and taut.

This second plumb line must be parallel to the horizontal plumb line. Check by measuring the distance between the two lines at several places. If the measurement is exactly the same at each point, your lines are parallel. If there is a discrepancy, recheck and adjust until the plumb lines are parallel. Notice that the upper plumb line does not follow evenly on the horizontal strip as your horizontal plumb line does. That is because fabrics tend to stretch and realign themselves during the construction and quilting processes. The landscape's irregular quilting can be a major reason for this natural unevenness.

With care, place a yardstick or other measuring tool along this newly formed upper plumb line. Mark a straight line on the landscape precisely at the plumb line, using the straight edge as a guide. Do not stretch the fabric while marking.

MARKING THE LOWER HORIZONTAL PLUMB LINE

Next, find the lower plumb line. Determine the exact distance between the horizontal plumb line and your landscape's selected lower edge. Position your pins as you have previously. Then thread the pins in the figure-8 fashion. The line should be taut and straight. This is your lower horizontal plumb line.

Check the plumb line's accuracy. Make certain that it is parallel to the horizontal plumb line by measuring at several places along the line. If the line is parallel, mark in the same manner as before. This drawn line is the lower edge of your quilt. Thus, from

Figure 17.Plumb Line for Straightening Quilt

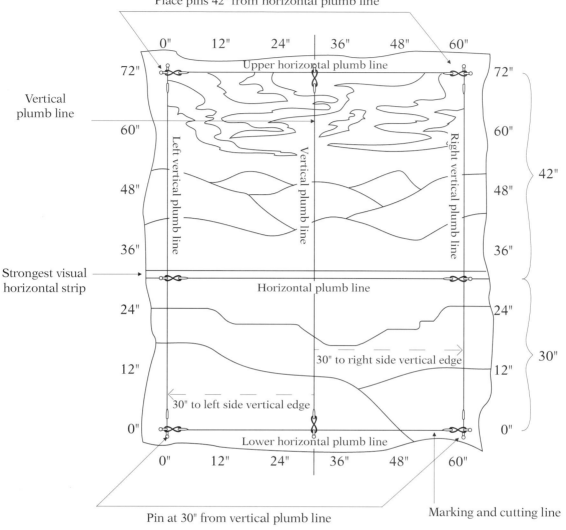

Place pins 42" from horizontal plumb line

0"   12"   24"   36"   48"   60"

72"   Upper horizontal plumb line   72"

Vertical
plumb line

60"   60"   } 42"

Left vertical plumb line   Vertical plumb line   Right vertical plumb line

48"   48"

36"   36"

Strongest visual
horizontal strip   Horizontal plumb line

24"   24"   } 30"

30" to right side vertical edge

12"   12"

30" to left side vertical edge

0"   Lower horizontal plumb line   0"

0"   12"   24"   36"   48"   60"

Pin at 30" from vertical plumb line   Marking and cutting line

the original horizontal plumb line you will have established the upper and lower edges of your landscape picture.

FINDING THE VERTICAL PLUMB LINE

Now you need to find the vertical plumb line. After determining this line, you will be able to establish and mark the two vertical sides of your landscape. To determine this plumb line, first place a large-headed pin at a point near the midpoint of the landscape's lower edge. The pin tip should face inward. This pin should be placed just below the marked lower edge line. Place the T square alongside the pin, perpendicular to the lower edge marking. Extend the T square's perpendicular line by using the

yardstick or meter stick. Overlap the two straight edges for at least eight inches to make sure that the extension continues to be perpendicular to the lower plumb line.

Attach the thread in figure-8 fashion to the pin at the lower edge. With thread in hand, go to the top edge of the landscape. Move the thread so that it lies exactly along the edges of the T square and other straight edge. Position a pin at the top edge of the landscape along the upper plumb line, facing inward. It should be precisely positioned so that the thread will remain alongside the two vertical straight edges. Place the thread around the pin. In position, the thread should be perpendicular to all three horizontal plumb lines. Check for accuracy. If correct, you have now established the vertical plumb line.

Figure 18. Figure-8 Pinning

Figure-8 pinning stabilizes plumb line thread.

MARKING SIDE VERTICAL PLUMB LINES

To find the left vertical plumb line, determine the exact distance desired between the vertical plumb line and the proposed left vertical side of your landscape. Place pins vertically at this distance intersecting both the upper and lower horizontal plumb lines. As done previously, attach the thread to both pins. Measure for accuracy. If the distance between the two vertical lines is the same throughout the entire left side, then the new plumb line is accurate. Redo if it is not correct. As you have done with the top and bottom edges, mark the left vertical plumb line.

Find the right vertical plumb line by first determining the desired distance between the vertical plumb line and the proposed right vertical side. Note that the distance between these two lines will not be the same as the distance from the vertical plumb line to the left side measurement unless your vertical plumb line divides the quilt precisely in half. Find the right plumb line in the same manner as you did for the left side. When the line has been accurately pinned, mark it. Your fourth and last side has been established with this right vertical plumb line.

FINISHING TIPS

Look at the edges of your landscape. Are they straight? Are the corners at 90 degree angles? If something seems incorrect, redo and then recheck. When you are satisfied that all sides are perfect, unpin all plumb lines. Carefully cut on the four marked edges of the landscape. When you are finished, you should have a landscape that has four perfectly straight, perpendicular sides.

After the quilt sides have been straightened, the finishing steps begin. For most situations, simply bind the landscape picture in your usual manner. The binding can be made of only one fabric, as is most common, or you can combine several fabrics into the binding, following the different colorations around the design. Whatever you decide, the binding should be subtle. The colors or fabrics should never distract from the landscape.

Since the binding is the first area to wear, consider doubling it. It is not necessary to make a binding from biased fabric unless your picture is curved. A simple binding can be made by cutting four strips, with each strip being approximately two inches longer than the quilt edge it will be attached to. Cut these strips three inches wide, then fold and press in half vertically. Sew the strips to the four sides of the landscape in parallel order, using a ¼-inch seam allowance. Hand sew the binding to the backing fabric with a blind hem stitch or other similar stitch. (For in-depth binding instructions, see Suggested Reading List in Appendix II.)

If you wish to have your landscape professionally framed, sew extensions to each side of the picture. Take the landscape to a professional framer—preferably one who has worked with fiber before. Have the framer stretch the picture. During the stretching process the landscape should not be pulled so tightly that the stitches show. The stretching should be gentle, used merely for further straightening and flattening. After stretching, the picture is framed. The type of framing material and the color of the frame should work well with the landscape hues.

You should be very proud of yourself when your landscape is completed, because you will have successfully created a visual work of art that includes many difficult steps. The mental process of visualization, the designing, construction, and quilting of the landscape picture, the selection of appropriate fabrics, and the well-planned application of color are all part of this challenging procedure. If you have given thoughtful attention to each of these integral parts of the total project, your landscape picture will almost certainly turn out to be as beautiful as you had imagined. Congratulations!

PART THREE

Creating Scenic Imageries

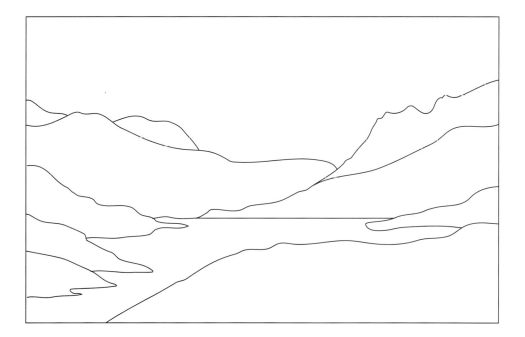

Chapter VIII
Designing Successful Landscapes

CONCEPT 1:
Using Our Environmental Influences

The influence of dwelling in a land of great beauty entwines itself forever in our lives and affects the way we interpret the world. A lifetime of visual memories lie deep within the recesses of our minds, waiting to be recaptured at a later date. Rather than deny these irrepressible environmental influences, let us embrace them and give them back to the world through visual artistic expression. If we are truly interested in our creative interpretations, we need to understand and accept our present and our past, and allow both to make an impact on us.

I grew up in a geographically isolated community of Seattle where the incongruous city setting was amplified by the steep wooded hills on three sides and Puget Sound with its glistening islands to the west. The quiet, picturesque neighborhood was idyllic: a wooded waterfront park, ferry boats slipping in and out of their moorings, quiet pebble beaches, the ever-present majestic Olympic Mountains across the waterway, breathtaking sunsets, and heavy blankets of fog on early winter mornings as a backdrop for the musical foghorns reverberating forlornly through the mist. Memories of my annual childhood sojourn to a pristine hideaway nestled in the wilderness of inner British Columbia include vivid images of sandy beaches, forests meeting the lakeside, and water dancing in the sunlight.

Now my home is on a tiny, rural island in southern Puget Sound. A pastoral view of water, hills, mountains, sunrises, and sunsets greets me daily in this setting, providing a simplistic, informal, serene atmosphere. Without conscious thought, my past and present are forever bound together, and my creative interpretations are undeniably a reflection of the two.

I invite you to use your own environmental uniqueness to rouse the artistic expressions within yourself. Whether your heart is in the southwest, the Appalachians, the prairies, the Rocky Mountains, New England, the Swiss Alps, the rolling hills of Ireland, the Cornish seacoast, the Great Barrier Reef, or somewhere else in this vast world, those inner environmental yearnings will help attune you to your intuitive creative nature. As a result, your subconscious mind will be better able to guide you to develop your own personal color and design style.

Creativity is always a risk, but it is easier if the focus has personal meaning. Therefore, when you create your landscape pictures, make them relevant to your life. Allow your inner soul a voice in your artistic expression by giving it the choice of the theme. When this happens, your visual impressions will be born.

As you formulate your ideas for creating a landscape, you can employ several basic guidelines to help ensure that your artwork will be meaningful to you and visually pleasing to the viewer. Before designing your scene, familiarize yourself with the following ideas that are vital to successfully designing a landscape picture. Of prime importance are attention to the focal point, the ability to promote depth perception to its fullest, and the recognition and use of nature's linear design qualities.

To help simplify the designing task, instructions on how to enlarge or reduce a design and directions for determining the size of your landscape have been included in this chapter. All information included in this chapter has been planned to be used as a working resource that you can easily refer to each time you begin a new landscape design.

CONCEPT 2:
Creating the Focal Point

As in any artwork, a landscape picture should have a focal point. There are two major types of focal points to consider. The first is very specific, being similar to the main character in a book. The picture is developed around one major design element or feature. Such a visual focal point could be Diamond Head, Mt. Shasta, a specific meadow, a flower garden, the moon, the sun shining on the water, a road, a cloud, or a specific land formation. (For examples, see photos 7, 19, 25, and 32.)

The other form of focal point is more generalized, but the focus is still very evident. This structure can

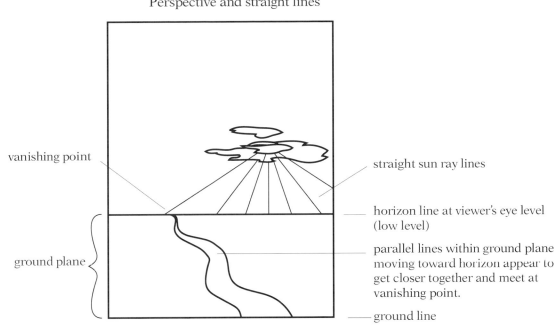

Figure 19.
Perspective and straight lines

vanishing point

straight sun ray lines

horizon line at viewer's eye level
(low level)

parallel lines within ground plane
moving toward horizon appear to
get closer together and meet at
vanishing point.

ground plane

ground line

be related to the main theme of a book, rather than the main character. This focus presents a broader spectrum of interest within the design. It generally encompasses most of the picture area. A range of mountains, an expansive view of meadowlands, a breathtaking sky or sunset, mistiness, the land formations of a desert—no one specific element stands out in single glory. Instead, the presentation is more comprehensive. (For examples, see photos 11, 16, 28, 29, and 44.)

Know which type of focal point you want to use. Then determine what your focal point will be. While you draw your design, plan how you will focus on your featured design element or main theme. When constructing the picture, make the focal point stand out in color, design, and composition so that the viewer is drawn to it.

After you determine your focal point, decide where it will be placed in the landscape picture. The focal point should not be at the midpoint of your picture, either horizontally or vertically. This is predictably elementary and generally makes the viewer feel that the focal point has been simply plopped into the picture. The illusion, then, is weakened or undone.

Instead, the focal point should be placed above or below the horizontal middle of the picture, and to the left or right of the vertical center. Play with your design and see where your focus works best visually.

While you are placing your focal point to its best advantage, remember that essentially you should attempt to design your scene as an open composition.

Your goal should be to allow the observer to feel that the landscape goes beyond the boundaries of the picture being viewed.

If you use a photograph as a guide for your composition, do not feel compelled to follow the design of the picture exactly. Move the focus of the picture, or even change the focus, if it will give you a better design.

For instance, you may be inspired by a photograph that focuses on a boat in the foreground waterway. Often a large percentage of area in these types of pictures is devoted to water. If your interest in the photo was because of a feature other than the boat, adjust the design to eliminate much of the water.

At other times a photograph may contain a great expanse of foreground and a small amount of sky. Unless your foreground has special interest, shorten this area if it is overly large. Conversely, the sky can be lengthened. You should look beyond the photographer's focus when using a photo as your design inspiration. Keep the parts of the design which you especially like and adjust for your own inclusions.

Lastly, delete anything in your design that is not absolutely essential. You may add features that enhance the landscape, but keep the focus of the picture simple. This simplicity gives visual clarity. It also makes construction easier. Many of the details that you may wish to include in your picture may be added during the quilting process rather than during construction.

Figure 20.
Enlarging a Design from Original Picture
Enlarging picure: 6" x 4" doubled = 12" x 8"

Original picture has
grid lines every ½ inch

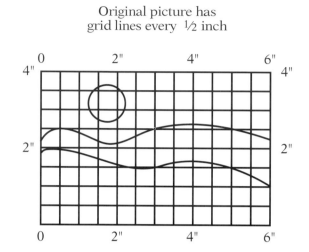

Making enlarged scale to redraw design
with grid lines every 1 inch

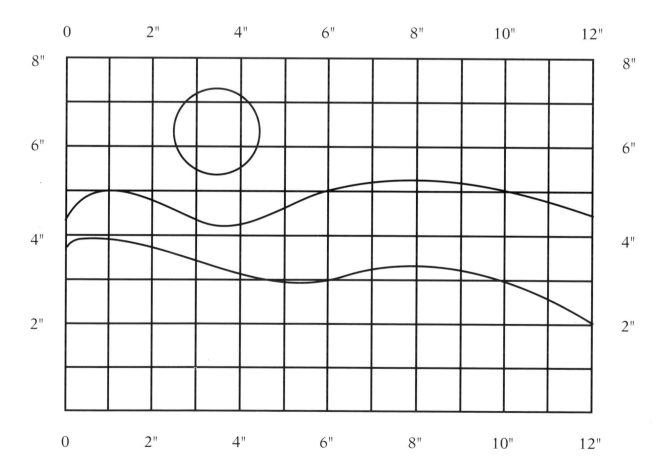

CONCEPT 3:
Using Linear Perspective in Nature

Your landscape picture can be greatly influenced by the use of linear design. Lines can emphasize design elements, provide details, and accentuate color or illusions. They can also be used to set a mood. Use linear design to increase the interest and beauty of your art.

Curved lines suggest a graceful or serene ambiance. Straight horizontal lines are restful. Vertical straight lines evoke power or strength. Angular lines can give a feeling of agitation, confusion, intensity, or interest. Diagonal lines suggest motion. You can use this knowledge to accentuate a psychological viewpoint that you wish to awaken in the viewer. (For examples of different emotive feelings through lines, see photos 6, 12, 25, 37, 38, and 45.)

Straight lines are rare in nature. Occasionally the sun's rays are seen as straight lines. These are actually created by atmospheric moisture. Another example of a straight line in nature is the horizon line. The only other straight lines that are usual in landscape pictures are perspective lines or the lines from manmade structures such as buildings. Keep straight lines out of your landscapes except when they represent a realistic interpretation of an actual setting.

Using color and perspective together gives you the ability to attain excellent depth in your landscape. Perhaps the greatest use of line perspective will be your quilting. Although most depth perception will be achieved with color, some knowledge of perspective is helpful when planning your design.

The straight horizontal line at the bottom edge of your picture is called the ground line. The horizon line is the most distant ground line in your picture. It runs parallel to the ground line. The area lying between the two lines is called the ground plane. (See Figure 19.)

The horizon line is always at the viewer's eye level. Therefore, if the eye level is high, the horizon level will be in the upper portion of the picture. If the eye level is low, the horizon line is in the lower portion of the picture.

Parallel lines within the ground plane which move toward the horizon appear to get closer together as they recede into the distance. Eventually they meet and seem to disappear on the horizon line. The point where they meet on the horizon line is called the vanishing point. Furrows, roads, pathways, and boundaries can all be included in your landscape through this form of perspective, which is called parallel perspective or one-point perspective.

To attain visual depth, the farther an object is from you, the smaller it becomes. For instance, mountains may be the same size, but as they recede into the distance they appear to decrease in size. The ones closest to you are the largest; those farthest away are the smallest. Likewise, trees in the foreground always appear larger than those in the distance, even though they may actually be the same size.

Remember that nature is our best resource for learning about lines in nature and linear perspective. Whenever possible, include in your landscape pictures types of perspective designs similar to those you observe in your natural surroundings.

CONCEPT 4:
Reducing and Enlarging the Design

If you do not draw your own design, you will probably need to enlarge, reduce, or trace the picture you have selected to use so that it can be made into a workable construction drawing. The size of your construction drawing should remain proportional to the original picture when you reduce or enlarge it. (See Figure 20.)

When you enlarge a picture, always multiply the original picture's length and width measurements by the same number to find the size of your construction drawing. To double a 3 inch x 6 inch picture, multiply 3 x 2 = 6 and 6 x 2 = 12. The size of your construction drawing would then be 6 inches x 12 inches.

If the original picture is 5 inches x 7 inches, double the size to 10 inches x 14 inches. If the original picture is only 3 inches x 4 inches, triple the size, making your drawing 9 inches x 12 inches. If you have a 2 inch x 4 inch picture, you may wish to enlarge it 2½ times. Thus, the construction drawing would be 5 inches x 10 inches.

If your original picture is too large to make a construction drawing from, reduce it to a manageable size. When you reduce the size of a picture, divide both the length and width side measurements by the same number. For example, if your picture is 24 inches x 17 inches and you wish to halve the size, divide the length and width each by 2. A 24 inch x 17 inch picture would be reduced to a 12 inch x 8½ inch construction drawing.

When the original picture is a workable size and it needs to be preserved, simply take tracing paper (preferably graph paper) and place it over the design. Trace all desired design elements. This, then, will be your construction drawing. All markings are then made on the tracing paper as you would any other drawing.

If the original picture is a workable size, and does not need to be saved, simply use it as your construction drawing. Place your grid lines directly on the picture along with all the other design markings.

CONCEPT 5:
Using Grid Lines

After you have drawn your construction drawing, you will need to make horizontal and vertical grid lines. These lines are used as references during the construction process. As a generalization, the grid lines in your construction drawing will almost always be in 1-inch increments. Variations are possible, however. If your drawing is on the small side, consider making your grid lines in ½-inch or ¾-inch increments. If your construction drawing turns out to be relatively large, the grid lines may be in 1½-inch increments. Grid lines are construction guides, so they need to be placed frequently to be of value. (See Part V, Landscape Patterns, for examples of construction drawings with grid lines.)

Grid lines can also be used to help transfer a design from the original picture to the construction drawing. If you are unsure of your drawing ability when transferring the design from the original picture to the construction drawing, make grid lines on both the drawing and the original picture. To do this, make the same number of grid lines in your original picture as the construction drawing has. Then draw the design, matching the design lines with the ones in the original picture, square by square. (See Figure 20.)

CONCEPT 6:
Determining Landscape Size

Before beginning construction of your piece, determine the landscape's proposed finished size. Keep the proportions of your landscape picture and the construction drawing the same. To determine the size of the landscape, multiply the width and height of the construction drawing by the same number until you reach a size that best fits your needs. The following are examples of landscape size options.

Example I:
Construction Drawing is 12" x 8"

Drawing consists of 1" grid line increments

2 x larger	24" x 16"	(12 x 2, 8 x 2) too small
2½ x larger	30" x 20"	1" on drawing = 2½" fabric
3 x larger	36" x 24"	1" on drawing = 3" fabric
4 x larger	48" x 32"	1" on drawing = 4" fabric

Example II:
Construction Drawing is 6" x 8"

Drawing consists of 1" grid line increments

4 x larger	24" x 32"	1" on drawing = 4" fabric
5 x larger	30" x 40"	1" on drawing = 5" fabric
6 x larger	36" x 48"	1" on drawing = 6" fabric
7 x larger	42" x 56"	1" on drawing = 7" fabric
8 x larger	48" x 64"	1" on drawing = 8" fabric

Example III:
Construction Drawing is 12" x 7 1/2"

Drawing consists of 1½" grid line increments
There are 8 horizontal increments
(12 divided by 1½ = 8)
There are 5 vertical increments
(7½ divided by 1½ = 5)
Multiply the increments 8 and 5 by proportional increases

4 x larger	32" x 20"	(8 x 4, 5 x 4)
5 x larger	40" x 25"	1 increment = 5" fabric
6 x larger	48" x 30"	1 increment = 6" fabric
7 x larger	56" x 35"	1 increment = 7" fabric

Extremely small landscapes are the most difficult to create with strip pieced landscape techniques. In the beginning, do not construct a piece that is less than 24 inches wide unless the design is very simple. For the same reason make the height at least 24 inches. For further simplification, stay within a 40-inch width so that your picture is no wider than the standard fabric yardage.

When you have determined the size of your landscape and how many inches each increment equals, mark the measurements at the grid lines on all four sides of your construction drawing.

PART FOUR

Exercises, Lessons, & Activities

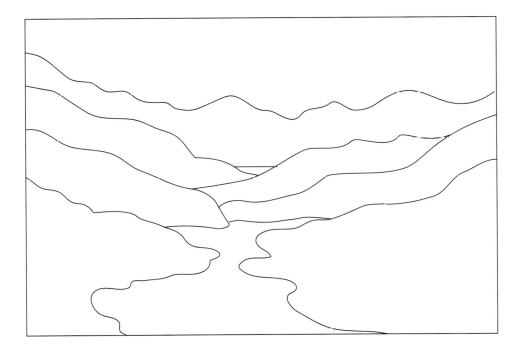

Chapter IX
Learning Strip Piecing Techniques

Chapter IX walks you through the sequential steps of the basic strip piecing landscape construction. After completing this section, you will have learned all the general techniques of folding and sewing strips of fabric together to attain a scenic design. It is best to become familiar with these technical skills before creating your first landscape.

This chapter includes the following exercises: 1.) basic folding method; 2.) changing the angle direction and the design position; 3.) using three or more fabrics in a horizontal strip; 4.) sewing strips together vertically into strip sets; 5.) using reference points with the V pinning method; 6.) creating mountains and valleys, and 7.) sewing ¼-inch-wide strips with precision.

To do these exercises, you will need the following:

threaded sewing machine and sewing tools
pins and fabric scissors
rotary cutter, mat, T square,
ruler or metal/plastic strips, 1½" wide and ¾" wide

Cut the following fabric strips:

1 or 2 strips of blue sky fabric, each 1½" wide
1 or 2 strips of green hill fabric, each 1½" wide,
1 strip of mountain fabric, 1½" wide
1 strip of blue or green fabric, ¾" wide,

Note: The number of fabric strips to be cut will depend on the amount of fabric you use for the various exercises. Make each completed strip in your exercises approximately 15 to 18 inches long. The completed exercise strips can be cut the finished length after the seams have been sewn. This avoids cutting any strips too short.

EXERCISE I: Basic Fold
1. Pick one sky fabric strip (strip A). Place this fabric horizontally on the work surface. Because the sky is visually in the background, it will remain unfolded. (See below.)

2. Pick out one hill fabric (strip B). On the left hand side of the strip, hand press a fold that is angled toward the right. If the fabric does not easily hold a fold, press with an iron. Leave at least a 2-inch to 3-inch tail at the folded end of this strip. Notice that with this particular directional fold, the tail falls to the bottom of the strip. (See below.)

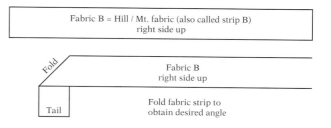

3. Place the folded fabric onto the background fabric with both strips running horizontally. Position the folded strip on the right hand side of the sky strip. Let several inches of your sky strip overlap horizontally behind the folded top strip. It is important that both fabric strips remain on a horizontal plane when they are in this initial phase. (See below.)

4. With both strips in place, gently open up strip B so that the wrong side is now facing up. The fold line has now become a crease. Position the crease so that both of its ends meet at the edges of strip A. The two strips have now formed an outside angle with the vertexes positioned at the crease line. (See below.)

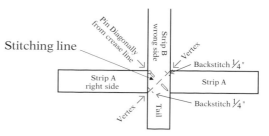

Keeping the crease line in place, carefully pin the two strips together. The pin should be placed diagonally with the crease line. When properly pinned, the two should form an X. This will stabilize the strips as well as allow you to see the crease line while sewing the seam. Sew the two strips together on the crease. Begin and end the seam by backstitching ¼ inch.

It is essential that the stitching goes into each vertex when beginning and ending the seam. If for some reason the crease has shifted out of position and does not end at one or both vertexes, sew the seam by eye, making certain that you sew into each vertex.

5. After sewing, check the completed strip by placing it horizontally on the work surface. Examine to see if the seams match the desired angle. Observe if both strips are going in a horizontal direction. (See below.) If, after being sewn, strip B is in a vertical setting rather than a horizontal one, it was incorrectly placed on strip A during the third step. Either rip out or cut out the seamed area and begin again.

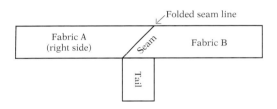

6. If you are satisfied with the sewn strips, cut off the excess tail fabric, leaving a ¼-inch seam allowance. At the same time, cut off the excess strip of the background fabric A, also leaving a ¼-inch seam allowance. (See drawing below.)

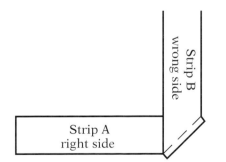

7. Place the finished strip right side up on the table. It should look similar to the drawing below.

EXERCISE II:
Changing Angle Direction and Design Position

8. With two more fabrics, strip A being sky and strip B as the hill, complete another angle. However, turn the angle toward the left, still using the left end of strip B. Again, place it on the right side of the sky strip. For this angle, the tail will be positioned at the top of the strips. (See below.)

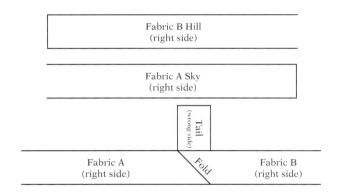

Open up the folded fabric carefully, as you did before. Pin in place by matching the crease line to the vertexes. Sew from vertex to vertex. Cut excess fabric and tail.

Now sew the two completed strips together, not worrying about matching fabric changes. When completed, you have begun your first strip set.

9. Build two more strips with strip A and B fabrics. Place the hill on the left hand side of strip A rather than the right. Consequently, strip B's fold will be made near its right hand edge. Angle the fold toward the left while positioning the folded strip on the left hand side of the sky strip. The strip B tail will be falling toward the bottom of the strip. (See drawing below.)

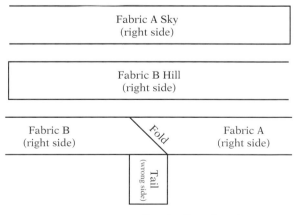

Exercise II continued on next page.

10. With the next set of strip A and B, angle the folded strip toward the right while still placing it on the left hand side of the sky strip. For this, the tail will be going above the strips. (See below.)

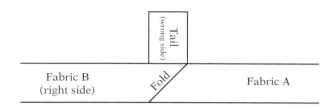

11. Notice that the angles of the folded strips can vary a great deal. The angle of each folded strip is determined by approximating the angle of the design element you are working with in the construction drawing. The direction of the fold is decided in the same manner and can be attained by folding angles in either the left or right direction. (See various angles below.)

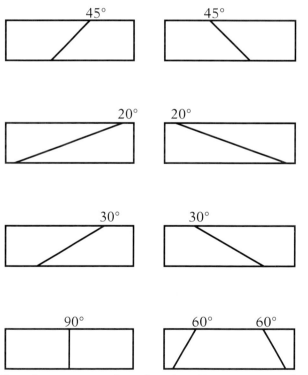

The above are samples of angles. Never measure the angles, simply make by visually matching the fold with the design element within the construction drawing. 90° angles are used for vertically straight elements like trees. 45° angles are used for combining strips for length, random color, or to attain design elements. 30 to 60° angles are used for steep sides—such as mountain tops. 20° or less angles are used for gentle slopes.

12. Make at least one strip using a very gradual angle, such as 20 degrees. (It is not necessary to measure angles; the calculations are done by eye.) When making a gradually angled seam, press the fold with an iron to set it well. As you position the folded strip onto the background fabric, you may want to use two to three pins to keep it in place. Sew from vertex to vertex, even if the crease line has moved. Cut off excess fabric and tails. Long, gradual angles are the most difficult ones to make. (See below.)

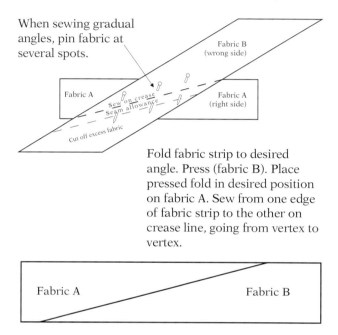

Fold fabric strip to desired angle. Press (fabric B). Place pressed fold in desired position on fabric A. Sew from one edge of fabric strip to the other on crease line, going from vertex to vertex.

View of sewn fabric strips.

EXERCISE III:
Making Strips with
Three or More Fabrics

13. Choose two green fabrics and one blue fabric to make a strip that will use three fabrics. First, in the usual manner sew two strips together, one hill and the sky fabric. Choose the direction of the hill angle and determine which side of the sky strip it will be located on. (See below.)

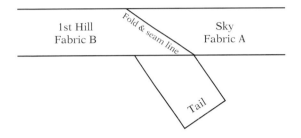

14. After the excess seam allowances and tails have been cut from the first seam, add the next fabric strip, the second hill, to the sky strip. This hill strip will be angled in the opposite direction from the first one. This third strip can be placed at any distance from the first hill. When you have sewn the three strips together, cut the excess fabric. (See below.)

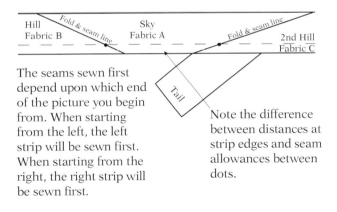

The seams sewn first depend upon which end of the picture you begin from. When starting from the left, the left strip will be sewn first. When starting from the right, the right strip will be sewn first.

Note the difference between distances at strip edges and seam allowances between dots.

When doing a picture, your construction drawing will dictate the distance between the hills. If you were to add another fabric strip to the horizontal design, this new fabric would be placed on the strip that is visually just beneath it.

EXERCISE IV:
Sewing Strips Together Vertically,
Using Reference Points,
and the V Pinning Method

Note: Most seams will not have designs that have to be matched precisely from one strip to the next. Generally, they can be staggered from ¼ inch to several inches, depending on the design. When figuring out where to join the strip set with the newly completed horizontal strip, keep in mind that you have to allow for the seam allowance adjustment.

15. Reference points are exact intersections where two design elements meet on adjacent strips. You must consider the seam allowances when determining where these reference points will intersect along the seam line. (See below.)

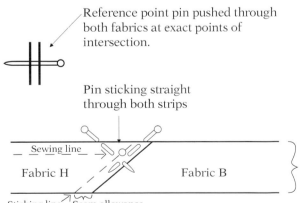

16. Select two completed strips with fabric changes that can be used as reference points. Place both strips together with right sides facing each other. Put the reference pin into each strip at the exact point where you want the design changes to meet. With the pin sticking straight through the two strips, take the other two pins and position them into a V, surrounding the reference pin. (See below.)

Reference point pin pushed through both fabrics at exact points of intersection.

Pin sticking straight through both strips

Sewing line

Fabric H   Fabric B

Stiching line   Seam allowance

Sew to first pin; take pin out; sew to reference point pin. Take pin out; sew over pin hole from reference point pin; take out last pin, and continue sewing along seam line.

Sew the strips together. At this time, the reference pin will be wiggling around. Try not to let it fall out of position before it should be pulled out. While sewing along the seam line, take out the first pin as you come to it. As the needle nears the reference pin, take it out carefully. Sew directly over the pin hole; pull out the last pin. Continue sewing along the seam line until the strips have been completly sewn together.

17. You may have more than one reference point to join between two adjacent strips. It is easiest to sew these points with precision when the new strip is being constructed, from reference point to reference point, at the same time as the two strips are being sewn together. Therefore, prepare and sew through the first reference point area as described in step 16. Then continue sewing along the seam line until the sewing needle is positioned about three inches from the next reference point. Stop sewing, backstitch, and cut away loose threads. (See below.)

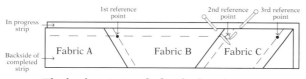

The back strip is only finished to the second reference point. After both strips are sewn together at the second reference point, the next fabric will be attached to the in-progress strip.

18. Position, pin, and sew the next folded fabric to be added onto the in-progress strip. Its exact placement is determined by the construction drawing. Sew the strips together. Cut off the excess fabric.

Next, pin the in-progress strip to the completed strip. At the second reference point, carefully V pin. Sew as before. Continue in this manner until all reference points have been sewn. (See below.) Then pin and sew the remainder of the seam line.

Reference points in completed strips

19. If your first reference point is quite far from the landscape edge, begin sewing the seam about 2 inches from the first reference point. Continue sewing your strip as previously described. When you get to the end of the seam line, turn the strip set over. Sew the seam line from where you started previously to the end of the unsewn side of the strip. Be sure to backstitch where the two stitching lines meet. (See below.)

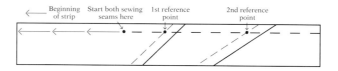

When the seam is completed, flip the strip set over, begin at the starting place—backstitch and proceed to the strip edge.

EXERCISE V:
Making Mountains and Valleys:

20. Mountain peaks and valleys are made identically. Look at the drawing. If you observe it in one direction, the picture is of two mountain peaks. If you turn the picture upside down, it looks like two valleys. (See below.) For verbal clarity this exercise will use mountains as its example, rather than valleys.

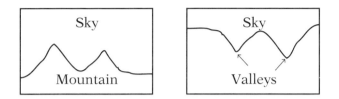

21. Sew the mountain fabric onto the sky fabric in the usual manner. When you are working on an actual design, make certain that the angle of the mountain is identical to the one in your construction drawing. After sewing, cut off excess fabric and press the seam line so that it lies flat. (See below.)

22. Using a second strip of sky fabric, fold it into the exact angle of the other side of the mountain. Place this sky strip on top of the sky-mountain strip. During actual construction, you would position this strip at the location which best corresponds to the construction drawing. If you want the top of the peak to end exactly at the seam line, position the second sky fabric so that it intersects the mountain-sky fabric strip line exactly where the strips will meet at the seam allowance. (See below.)

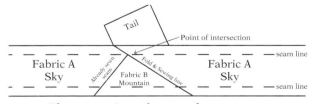

The mountain peak meets the seam line exactly.

23. If you would like a mountain with a flat top, locate the second sky fabric so that the two mountain fabrics do not intersect at the seam line. The flat top can be narrow or wide, depending on the placement of the second sky fabric. The seam line will become the summit of the flat top mountain. (See below.)

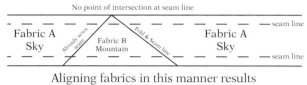

Aligning fabrics in this manner results in a flat top mountain.

24. If you would like the mountain peak to fall within the finished width of the strip, overlap the second sky fabric so that it intersects the first mountain-sky side somewhere below the projected seam line. (See below.)

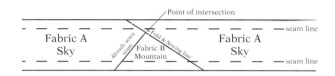

In this drawing, the peak fits between seam lines. It is the easiest to construct of all mountain peaks. Fabric strips should be at least 1½" wide to have large enough peak.

When making mountain tops, it is important to calculate where the seam allowance is going to meet the mountain fabric on the lower edge of the strip. It is easy to misjudge the needed width when the seam allowances are not considered. When this happens, there is usually too much difference between the mountain peak and the mountain section of the adjoining strip.

EXERCISE VI:
Sewing ¼-inch wide strips with precision

If you sew a ¼ inch finished strip to another using the conventional sewing methods, you will find that the strip's finished width is uneven while the seam allowances are straight. To make the finished width even, you need to use a different seam guide. For this technique, do the following:

25. Sew a ¾ -inch-wide strip to a hill or sky strip. (See below.)

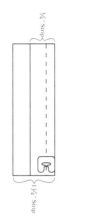

Sew ¾" wide strip to the adjacent strip in normal procedure.

26. Then proceed to add another sky or hill fabric strip to the strip set. To do this, first position the unsewn strip so that it lies underneath the ¾ inch strip. In doing this, you will have the back side of the strip set facing upward so that you can clearly see the first seam line of the ¾ inch strip. Pin the two strips together, continuing to keep the backside of the ¾ inch strip facing you. (See below.)

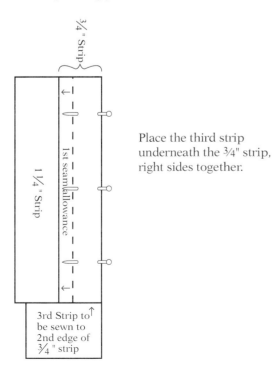

Place the third strip underneath the ¾" strip, right sides together.

27. With the sewing machine, begin sewing the seam. Do not use the conventional method of guiding your fabric while sewing. Instead, use the left side of your presser foot as your guide, abutting it to the first seam of the ¾ inch strip as you sew. (See below.)

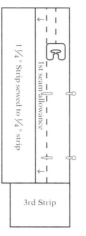

When sewing the second seam of a ¾" strip, use the left hand side of your presser foot as the seam guide. The left side of the presser foot should abut the first seam line as you sew. This will allow for the perfect ¼" finished strip on the finished side.

When the seam is completed, check for strip width accuracy on the front side of the strip set. Notice that the ¼-inch-wide strip will be straight, but on the reverse side the last seam allowance will be uneven. If you had sewn in the conventional manner, the seam allowance would be perfect, but the finished strip width would be irregular.

Because it is necessary to use the left seam line as the sewing gauge for ¼ inch precision sewing, you cannot be concerned with which end of the strip set you should begin sewing from at this time. However, begin alternating sides as soon as you add another strip to the set which is wider than ¼ inch.

Summary:

If there are any exercises or concepts that you did not finish successfully or did not completely understand, do another practice session from those particular areas of concern. After completing this chapter you should be able to fold and sew strips together using numerous angled positions while changing direction locations. You can probably make valleys and mountains as well, using any of the three special techniques. Also, you ought to be able to attach one completed strip to another, at certain times using the V pinning method for matching reference points precisely. Lastly, the ¼ inch precision sewing method should be familiar to you so that you will feel comfortable using narrow strips in your picture.

You are now ready to extend your practical experience by working through the lessons in Chapter X. During construction of your first landscape, use your practice strips as references until you become comfortable working with the techniques.

Chapter X
Lessons In Landscapes

INTRODUCTION:
Concepts And Supply Lists

This chapter is designed to give you the opportunity to experiment with color, design, and techniques through lessons and activities. Each lesson includes major subject references so that you can refer back to the relevant text for help or for a review of a particular topic.

Visual depth and luminosity are experimented with in the first three lessons. Lesson 4 takes you through the entire sequential process of creating a strip pieced landscape, from designing to binding. Other lessons and activities are provided for further understanding and learning.

Because information, concepts, and technical skills needed to complete these lessons are not discussed in this chapter, it is important for you to be familiar with the subject matter in the text and to have worked through the technical applications of strip piecing in Chapter IX before beginning.

For your convenience, the general supplies needed for the different steps in creating a landscape picture are listed below:

1. Designing the construction drawing:

1/4" graph paper	pencil
eraser	colored pencils
ruler	optional: tracing paper

selection of scenes from cards, magazines, photos, etc.

2. Constructing the landscape:

sewing machine	sewing machine equipment
rotary cutter	assorted colors of thread
cutting mat	24" T square
fabric scissors	seam ripper
iron/ironing board	extra-fine, extra-long pins
2 large-headed pins	

metal/plastic strips or ruler for strip width measurement

wide assortment of fabric, approximately ⅛ - ¼ yard each

3. Basting the landscape top to the backing and batting:

batting	backing material
masking tape	sharp needle
scissors	thread
teaspoon	thimble

4. Quilting the landscape picture: (*machine quilting)

scissors	hoop/frame

marking tool (chalk, pencil, etc)

extension fabric

high quality sewing thread or quilting thread

betweens/quilting needles, size 9 recommended

sewing machine and walking foot*

fine sewing machine needles*

clear nylon thread*

5. Straightening and finishing the landscape picture:

large-headed pins	top-stitching thread
T square	yard stick or meter stick
scissors	chalk or marking tool
binding fabric	iron/ironing board
sewing machine	thread/needle/thimble

LESSON #1
Creating Visual Depth

Objective:

After completing this lesson, you will have gained further understanding of visual depth and how it is achieved with fabric.

Set:

By making a mock-up with paper and scrap fabric, you will create a small picture illustrating visual depth.

References:

Visual depth: Chapter III, page 9

Time: 30 to 60 minutes

Supplies and Tools:

drawing paper	ruler
pencil	drafting triangle
glue stick	eraser
assorted fabrics	fabric scissors

Directions:

1. With a pencil, ruler, and drafting triangle, draw a 5 inch x 7 inch rectangle on your drawing paper.

2. In the rectangle, draw a simple scene that includes the following:

foreground	background
middle distance element(s)	sky

3. Choose materials to be used for each area of your picture. Place fabrics for each design element in separate stacks.

4. Select and cut fabrics to fit into the design elements. Glue the fabrics to your paper drawing as you work. (Fabrics do not have to be cut into strips for placement.)

Monitor and Adjust:

Place your completed picture on a wall. Study it from a distance. If it looks realistic, you have been successful in achieving visual depth. If a design element or fabric is "pulling out" of the design, make necessary changes. Correct any other areas that you think may be distracting.

Extended Learning:

1. Do the same lesson using one of the more complex patterns included in Part Five, Landscape Patterns, pages 73-82.

2. When you design your first landscape picture, make a fabric mock-up showing visual depth. Use colors in the mock-up similar to those you plan for your fabric landscape.

3. Begin a file folder that includes examples of pictures showing visual depth. This will be a good reference for future landscape projects.

Summary:

In addition to the objectives of this lesson, if you have worked through the extended learning section, you should be able to project visual depth within any landscape picture you create.

LESSON #2
Creating Luminosity

Objectives:

Completing this lesson will give you experience in working with toned fabrics in a prescribed manner so that you can create luminosity.

Set:

With a mock-up of paper and fabric, you will create a simple picture that includes a luminous design element.

References:

Tones:	Chapter I, page 4
Luminosity:	Chapter III, page 9-10
Time:	45 to 75 minutes

Supplies and Tools:

drawing paper	pencil
ruler	eraser
fabrics	fabric scissors
glue stick	drafting triangle

Directions:

1. With ruler, pencil, and drafting triangle, make a 5 inch x 8 inch rectangle on your drawing paper.

2. Draw a simple landscape that includes foreground, middle distance, background, and sky. In addition, place a sun or moon in your picture.

3. Carefully select the fabrics for your luminous object. Then choose the adjacent ones. Cut and place the materials in position. When you are satisfied with the illusion, glue in place.

4. Select the remaining sky fabrics. Cut, place, and glue them onto your drawing.

5. Choose fabrics for the rest of the picture. Continue to cut and place the fabrics on the drawing. Glue the fabrics in place.

Monitor and Adjust:

After completing your luminous scene, place it on a wall. Look at the picture from a distance. If you can see the sun or moon glowing, you have been successful. If the illusion is lost, or not readily seen, determine which fabrics did not work in the illusion. Change the necessary materials.

Extended Learning:

1. Repeat the same fabric experiment, choosing a design from Part Five, Landscape Patterns. Place a sun or moon in the design. Make it glow through fabric placement.

2. Create a luminous picture that will not use colors commonly attributed to the object's glow. For instance, do not make a yellow sun or a white moon. Attempt to obtain your luminous effect by using unusual colorations while still applying the rules for luminosity.

3. Begin a file collection of luminous scenes.

Summary:

If you successfully worked through the extended learning exercises in addition to the basic lesson, you should feel quite comfortable incorporating luminosity into any of your fabric landscape pictures.

LESSON #3
Creating Visual Depth In Fabric

Objectives:

While creating a simple fabric landscape, you will use color as the only element to show land, sky, and visual depth. Through this lesson you will experience the power of color in a design.

Set:

With only the two elements of land and sky, you will construct a strip pieced landscape. Visual depth will be obtained primarily by placing the darkest sky colors at the top of the picture and the lightest ones at the horizon line. In addition, if you are using prints for the land, you will position them to achieve the greatest visual depth.

References:

Photo reference:	Country Evening, photo 6
Visual depth:	Chapter III, page 9
Print fabric:	Chapter IV, pages 13-14
Construction:	Chapter V, pages 16-21
Time:	2 to 3 hours

Supplies and Tools:

sewing machine	sewing tools and supplies
rotary cutter	iron and ironing board
mat	T square
measuring tools	thread
scissors	sky and land fabrics

Directions:

1. Using the drawing at right, determine what the land will represent. With your sky design, decide the mood or time of day. (You may adjust the dimensions of the drawing.)

2. Choose the fabrics for the sky. Place them in an order that includes the lightest coloring at the horizon line and the darkest hues at the top of the picture. Set these fabrics aside.

3. Choose the land fabrics. Place them in an order that will best promote visual depth.

4. Following the construction procedures in Chapter V, cut your land strips in a variety of widths. Sew them together, working through the entire land area. When you have completed the land segment, press and staystitch around the perimeter. Set the land segment aside.

5. Begin constructing the sky, starting at the horizon line; continue to work in an upward progression. Vary the width of the strips. Try to use at least one ¼-inch finished strip. When you have completed the sky, press and staystitch around its perimeter.

Modify and Adjust:

Hang the two segments together on a wall as if they were one piece. Look at the picture from a distance. If you need to change any fabric strips or adjust the length of either segment, do so now. When you are satisfied with both segments, sew them together. Press. Do a preliminary straightening.

Extended Learning:

If you want to make this landscape into a finished picture, review as needed the chapters on basting, quilting, and straightening techniques. Hang the scene back on the wall. Try to visualize how you would use quilting stitches to enhance the design and to create more visual depth. After you have determined how you will quilt, begin basting, quilting, straightening, and finishing.

Summary:

By doing this lesson, you will have learned a great deal about color interaction within a landscape. You will also have had the experience of creating a simple fabric picture before beginning a more difficult design.

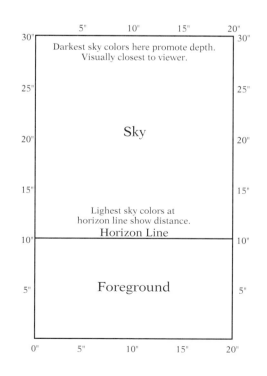

LESSON #4
Making A Strip Pieced Landscape

Objectives:

If you have read the main text and have practiced the strip piecing techniques in Chapter IX, you are ready to begin designing and constructing a strip pieced landscape.

Set:

This lesson has been broken into eight parts: 1.) preparing the construction drawing; 2.) selecting fabrics; 3.) constructing the first segment; 4.) continuing construction; 5.) basting; 6.) marking and quilting; 7.) straightening; 8.) finishing. Each step has been divided by concept, skill, or activity, rather than by any time relationship.

Whether you are working through these mini-lessons alone, as a group, in a class, or as an instructor, keep within the eight lesson divisions to simplify learning. If you need further information while working through these steps, refer back to the specific chapter that deals with the subject matter. A list of relevant references is provided below.

References:

Accepting environmental influences:	Chapter VIII, page 48
Reducing and enlarging the design:	Chapter VIII, page 51
Grid lines:	Chapter VIII, page 52
Determining the landscape size:	Chapter VIII, page 52
Using prints:	Chapter IV, pages 13-14
Visual depth:	Chapter III, page 9
General construction techniques:	Chapter V, pages 16-21
Strip piecing techniques:	Chapter IX, pages 54-60
Basting and quilting techniques	Chapter VI, pages 22-25
Straightening and finishing hints	Chapter VII, pages 43-45

Supplies and Tools:

Basic drawing supplies are listed on page 61.

Basic sewing supplies are listed on page 61.

Construction Hint:

When constructing the landscape, put a yardstick or other measuring tool on the edge of your work surface to keep track of the horizontal measurements of your fabric picture. You can also use a ruler for one of the vertical sides to help measure progress in height. (Masking tape marked in the same increments as the drawing can also be used.)

In addition, use a small ruler to plot your advancement on the construction drawing. Place the ruler so that its upper edge shows the horizontal line that you are working with. The ruler tends to clarify the horizontal strip design, making it easier to decide fabric placement and strip width determinations.

Directions: Work within the eight divisions of this lesson.

Part I: Preparing the Construction Drawing

1. Decide what landscape picture you would like to create. You can choose a drawing from Part V, Landscape Patterns, or make your own scenic design.

2. If you are using a design from this book, make your construction drawing by following the directions in Reducing and Enlarging the Design, Chapter VIII. If you need further help, see the drawings in Part V, Landscape Patterns, and also see page 16.

3. Color the construction drawing in hues similar to the ones you wish to use.

4. Put the grid lines in place vertically and horizontally. (See Grid Lines, Chapter VIII.)

5. Determine the size of your landscape. Figure out the ratio between the construction drawing and the landscape. Write in the incremental measurements at the edges of the construction drawing's grid lines. Mark them on all sides of the drawing. These grid line markings will allow you to make quick calculations between your drawing and your fabric landscape during the construction. (See Determining Landscape Size in Chapter VIII.)

6. Mark the segment divisions with horizontal dashes. See page 19.

Part II: Selecting Fabrics for the Landscape

1. Determine what special color effects you wish to include in your landscape. Decide the mood of your sky. Look at scenic picture books for color inspiration.

2. Choose the fabrics to be included in your picture. Then separate them into stacks, with each one representing a different design element. Set aside all but those to be used in the first segment. Upon beginning each new segment or design element, place the fabrics to be added on your work table; put away the ones you no longer need.

Part III: Constructing the First Segment

1. Prepare your work area for pressing, cutting, and sewing.

2. Study your drawing. Decide how wide you want to make the first strip, what fabrics will be needed in that strip, and where each fabric will be added horizontally.

Note: Remember that you will include 2-inch margins on both sides of your picture. Also, the first and last strips of the landscape are cut 1 inch wider for straightening purposes.

3. Press and straighten the fabric to be used on the first strip. Cut the strips the determined width, always adding ½ inch for seam allowances. Sew the fabrics together to form the first completed strip.

4. When you have completed the first strip, go on to the next, making certain that your fabric selection and horizontal placement relate to the strip just previously completed and to the construction drawing.

5. When you have finished piecing the first two horizontal strips, pin and sew them together. If the strips have to be joined at a precise location, do a V pinning at the reference points; sew in the prescribed manner. (See Chapter IX, Exercise IV, pages 57-58.)

6. Continue working by building each strip horizontally. As you complete a strip, join it to the previously completed one.

7. Work until you reach the segment division line. When you have completed the first segment, press it well. Do a preliminary straightening with the T square. Do not cut off the margins. Instead, keep the segment as wide as possible. Then staystitch the segment and set it aside.

Part IV: Continuing Construction

1. Begin the second segment in the design. Following the construction drawing, continue working upward through the design. Follow the drawing as closely as possible. Constantly vary the widths of your strips so that they are not in any set pattern.

2. When you have completed the second segment, prepare it as you did the first. Then sew it to the first segment. Set aside.

3. Begin the next segment of the design. Continue to work through the design, following the drawing closely.

4. When you have finished constructing all segments and have attached them all into one landscape piece, do a preliminary straightening, if needed. Press the landscape. Cut off any excess threads or fabric. Follow the directions at the end of Chapter V for preparing the top prior to basting.

Part V: Basting

After your top has been constructed, preliminarily straightened, pressed, and cleaned of excess threads, you are ready to baste. Follow the instructions in Chapter VI for basting the landscape picture.

Part VI: Quilting

1. Contemplate the type of quilting that you wish to include in your landscape. Review the suggestions for quilting lines in Chapter VI, pages 24-25.

2. Determine whether you will hand or machine quilt. Prepare your supplies accordingly. Mark and quilt the landscape, using the guidelines and suggestions in Chapter VI.

Part VII: Straightening the Landscape Picture

After the quilting process has been completed, straighten your quilt, using the modified plumb line technique. For detailed instructions, see Chapter VII.

Part VIII: Finishing the Landscape

Determine how you would like to finish the edges of your landscape picture. If you are going to bind the piece, use your favorite method. If you want to have your landscape framed, seek out a professional framer. (See page 45 for binding suggestions.)

Modify and Adjust:

1. As you proceed through the construction phase, you may find that you would like to simplify your design. Make changes as you think they are needed. For instance, you may decide to add more sky than your drawing indicates. You may also decide to take out an element or two. If you do not have to

stay within the confines of the drawing, making these changes is fine, as long as the end result is balanced with the rest of the landscape design.

2. When you finish each segment, place it on a wall with the other finished sections. Observe the progress from a distance. If there seems to be a problem with any of the fabrics or design elements, consider possible adjustments. However, do not act too quickly. Sometimes a fabric or design element will seem out of place when it is seen out of the complete context. When observed with the entire scene, it should work with the other fabrics to attain visual balance. In the end, if a fabric or element still pulls out of the total design, then make changes.

Extended Learning:

Assess the areas that you would like to explore further. In at least one area, increase the degree of difficulty of your next design. Also, consider working in a larger size. Encourage yourself to experiment with color use. Choose to do one of the following suggestions for your next landscape creation.

1. Create another landscape which incorporates a more difficult design than the one that you have just completed. Choose one of the patterns included in Part V, Landscape Patterns, or draw your own.

2. Construct a landscape that includes a luminous area. Use your Lesson 2 drawing, if you feel that it turned out quite well. See Chapter III for a review, if needed.

3. Create a landscape picture using a reflection as one of your major focal points. Review the general concepts of a reflection in Chapter III.

4. Design and construct a picture that encompasses the horizon line and linear perspective. This can be done through the construction design, the quilting design, or both processes.

5. Create a landscape picture that uses the partnership of a root color and its afterimage as its major color theme.

6. Continue collecting pictures for inspiration. As your experience grows, develop designs that are composites of some of these pictures.

Summary:

Congratulations! You have just accomplished a wonderful feat. Through the eight different steps in this lesson, you have successfully completed your first landscape picture. You are now on your way to making many beautiful fabric landscapes which echo your environmental impressions.

LESSON #5
Creating Luster

Objectives:

This is an optional lesson illustrating two different concepts. First, you will have the opportunity to use the Seminole technique to attain luster. You will also acquire a better understanding of how this process can be used for other design elements, such as flower gardens.

Set:

Using the accompanying pattern, construction, and technical drawings, you will create a landscape picture which will encompass luster.

Photo references:

Luster using Seminole method:	Photo 24
Seminole fabric for bulb fields:	Photo 21

References:

Luster reference:	Chapter III, pages 10-11
Shades, tone references:	Chapter I, pages 3-4
Time:	1 to 5 days
Supplies and Tools:	See general list on page 61.

Directions:

1. Determine whether your picture will contain a sun or a moon. From that decision, choose the fabrics to use in the different design elements in the picture. (See the drawing below.)

2. Line up the fabrics to be used for the lustrous illusion, going from the area of greatest glow to the darkest shimmer.

3. Choose the fabric to be the central focus within the lustrous area. This center fabric will be the one with the highest value of the gradated fabrics. Cut one strip from this particular fabric.

4. From each of the other fabrics chosen for the lustrous yardage, cut two strips. Cut the strips in varying widths as shown in the drawing. (See Figure 21.)

5. Place the center fabric strip on your work surface. Working outwards from the center, put the other fabrics in their order of gradation, going from lightest to darkest or from lightest to most toned. The fabrics on either side of the center strip will be the same. For a symmetrical effect, strips of the same fabric should be the same width. However, if you are interested in an asymmetrical effect, you may change the widths of some of the fabric partners.

Pattern for Shimmering Sun (See photo 24.)

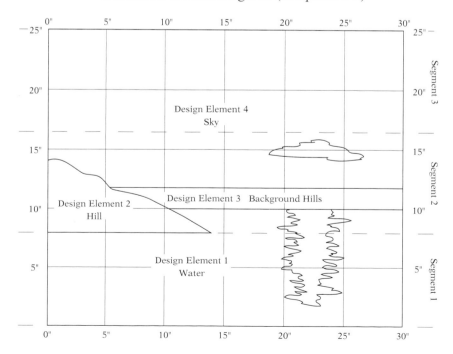

Figure 21. Seminole Piecing for Luster

Step One: Cut and place lustrous fabrics in order—highest value in the middle. Work outward to fabrics of lowest value. Sew fabrics to make your own fabric yardage.

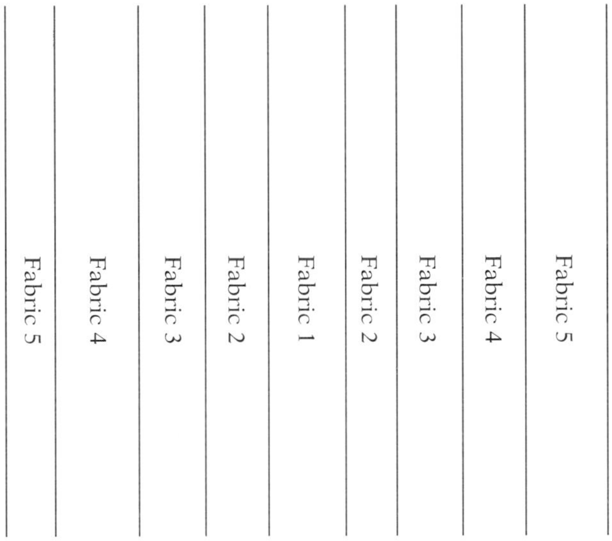

Fabric 5 | Fabric 4 | Fabric 3 | Fabric 2 | Fabric 1 | Fabric 2 | Fabric 3 | Fabric 4 | Fabric 5

Figure 22.

Step Two: Cut sewn fabric in strips in widths to match strips in your picture. Stagger their position within the horizontal strips to get a shimmering effect.

Strips of lustrous fabric are cut in assorted widths to be placed with water fabric.

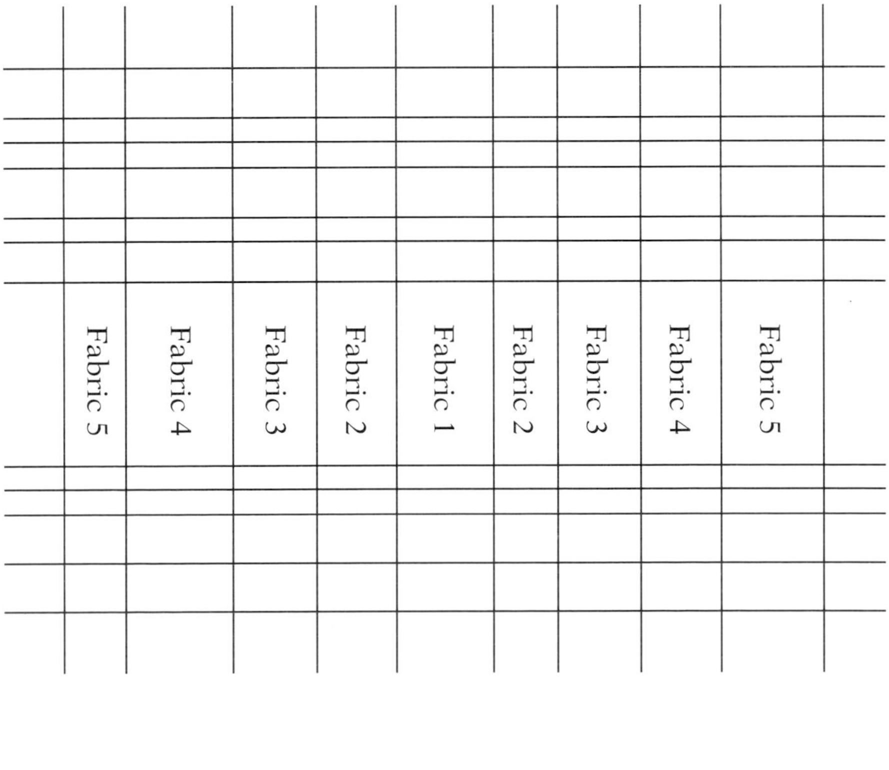

Fabric 5 | Fabric 4 | Fabric 3 | Fabric 2 | Fabric 1 | Fabric 2 | Fabric 3 | Fabric 4 | Fabric 5

6. After you have placed the fabric strips in the desired order, sew them together. Remember to alternate starting ends.

7. Press the finished strip set from both the front and back sides. Trim off excess threads and fabric.

8. The lustrous fabric for the shimmering effect has now been created. Straighten the edges of the newly made fabric so that they are perpendicular to the horizontal strips. Use a T square for accuracy.

9. Begin working on your landscape, starting at the bottom. When the luster is to be incorporated in the design, cut a strip of your lustrous fabric the same width as the horizontal strip it will be sewn to. (See Figure 22). Next, place and sew the lustrous strip on the water strip. Finish sewing the horizontal strip by adding the next fabric strip.

10. Cut the shimmering fabric strips one at a time so that they coincide in size to the horizontal strip they will fit into. As illustrated in the picture Shimmering Sun, vary the length of each lustrous strip by cutting or adding to the pieced strip. Also stagger the shimmering strip fabric in its vertical placement so that it is more realistic in effect. Work through the lustrous effect until it ends in your drawing.

11. Continue constructing the landscape following the design. When the top has been completed, finish all other steps as suggested in Lesson #4.

Modify and Adjust:

While incorporating the lustrous fabrics into your design, occasionally place the picture on a wall and observe it from a distance. Are you staggering the lustrous strips enough within each horizontal strip? Can some be staggered more? If the luster looks realistic, continue working as you have been. If the lustrous strips are too much in line vertically, consider changing a few of those strips by making the luster either longer or shorter horizontally.

Extended Learning:

1. Create a picture illustrating a different lustrous scene. Try to make the picture different from the previous one.

2. Attempt a winter scene with the moonlight falling on snow.

3. Create a scene with city lights falling on an ice pond or a body of water.

4. Use Seminole-type fabric to create a special effect within a landscape that does not involve luster, such as a flower garden or meadowland.

Summary:

Knowing how to use Seminole piecing to construct new fabric will give you additional skills to create color illusions. It will also allow you to increase your design capabilities with perspective through manipulating the fabric strip further.

ACTIVITY 1
Promoting Individual Color Visualization

1. Begin building files which illustrate different natural settings. Using books, magazines, advertisements, calendars, photographs, and other printed matter, start collecting pictures to put in these files. Study pictures to increase your understanding of color in nature. Use these examples for guidelines when creating your own landscape artwork.

Also, these examples of nature are helpful resources when creating artwork in other techniques.

Suggested file folder divisions are:

sunrises	sunsets
clouds	water
mountains	deserts
meadows	hills
forests	trees
mist	snow
flowers	storms
farm lands	leaves
rocks	beaches
daytime skies	fog

2. Set up a file folder for each season of the year. In these folders, place pictures, impressions, colorations—anything that gives you subtle clues or obvious examples of the different seasons. Use these files for study and for inspiration.

ACTIVITY #2
Promoting The Understanding Of Illusions

Make file folders which include examples of color illusions that you can use in landscapes. Collect these samples from magazines, books, calendars, cards, and other printed materials. Use them for references when creating your own pictures. Your files should include examples of:

depth	luminosity
luster	shadows
highlights	reflections
sunlight on objects	sky reflecting on water

other objects reflecting on water

shadows falling on hills, mountains, and rocks

ACTIVITY #3
Assessing Past Fabric Selections

1. Do you have fabrics in your collection which never seem to fit into your projects? Are there fabrics which you have had for years and yet have never found a place for? If so, there is a good possibility that these fabrics have design or color problems. Take out several of these fabrics from your collection. Analyze their characteristics. Categorize them into groups which may include any of the following:

a. large static geometric designs

b. other prints which take on a dominant role because of their strong design characteristics

c. prints with a pure white background in inappropriate settings

d. prints with too many colors

e. prints with no dominant color

After examining your collection of difficult fabrics, do you find a recurring pattern of selection? Are you choosing fabrics which consistently fit into one or two particular groups? If so, be aware of this selection problem on your fabric buying trips.

2. Look at your collection of fabrics again. Notice the scale of your fabrics. Do you lean toward paisley prints, large prints, medium-scaled prints, or small-scaled prints? Do you tend to choose dots, geometric designs, checks, stripes, or floral designs? Remember that you want to use a variety of scale in your fabrics. In addition, you also need to vary the types of patterns. For instance, don't just pick floral designs or geometric patterns. Use as many different types of designs as possible to fit your picture.

3. Look at your past quilts or fabric art. Have some projects had disappointing results? If so, attempt to analyze the problem. Have you used any of the fabrics mentioned above? If so, did they have a negative effect on the total visual image? Have you varied the scale of the fabrics used? Be aware of your past choices and how you would like to change them.

4. When you shop for fabric, make a deliberate attempt to eliminate buying patterns which result in choices that are detrimental to your artwork. It takes time to change buying habits that have developed over several years. When fabric shopping, it's easiest if you decide before you enter the store what types of fabrics you will look for. Then, if you change your mind about fabric selection in the store, you can consciously decide whether you have made a great spontaneous decision or whether the choice is based on habit.

PART FIVE

Landscape Patterns

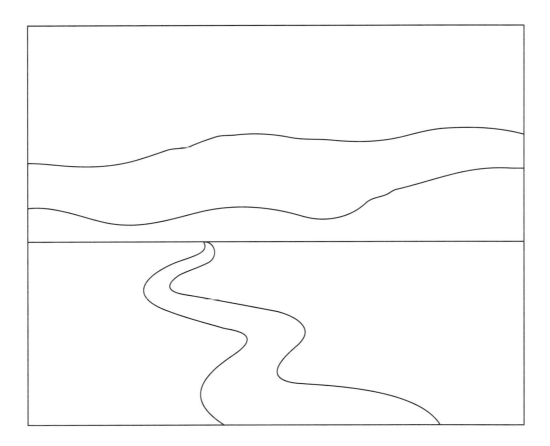

1. Country View

Size: 32" wide by 40" high

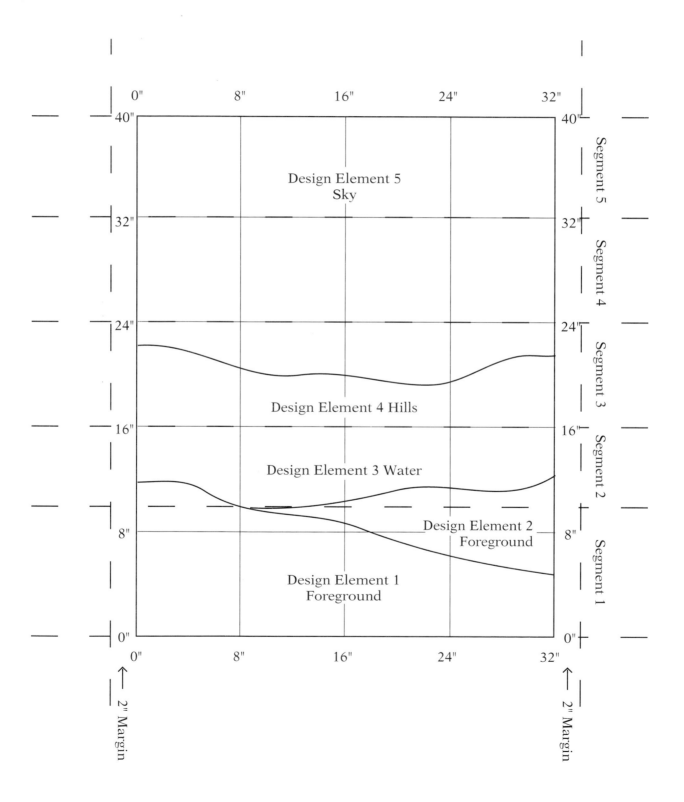

2. *Mountain Glow*

Size: 42" wide by 48" high

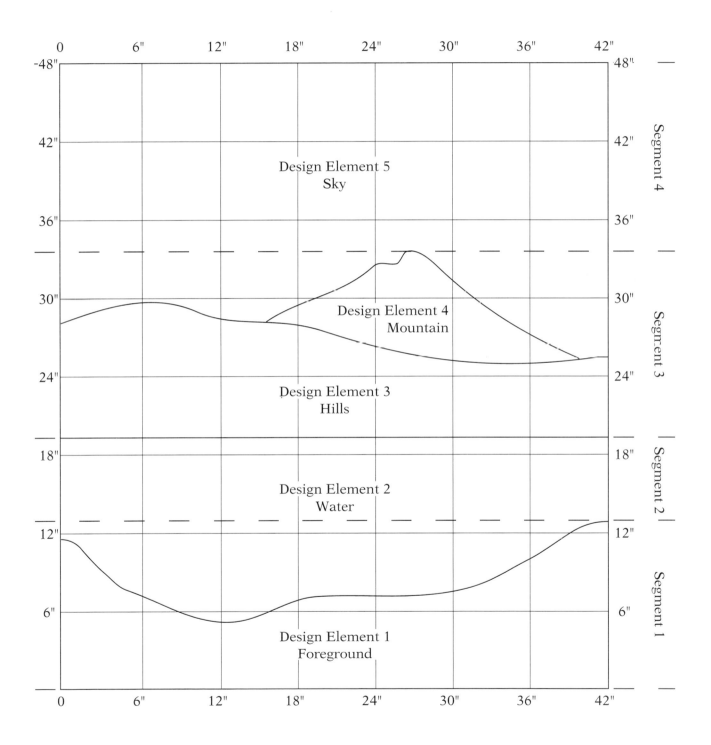

3. Country Calm

Size: 25" wide by 45" high

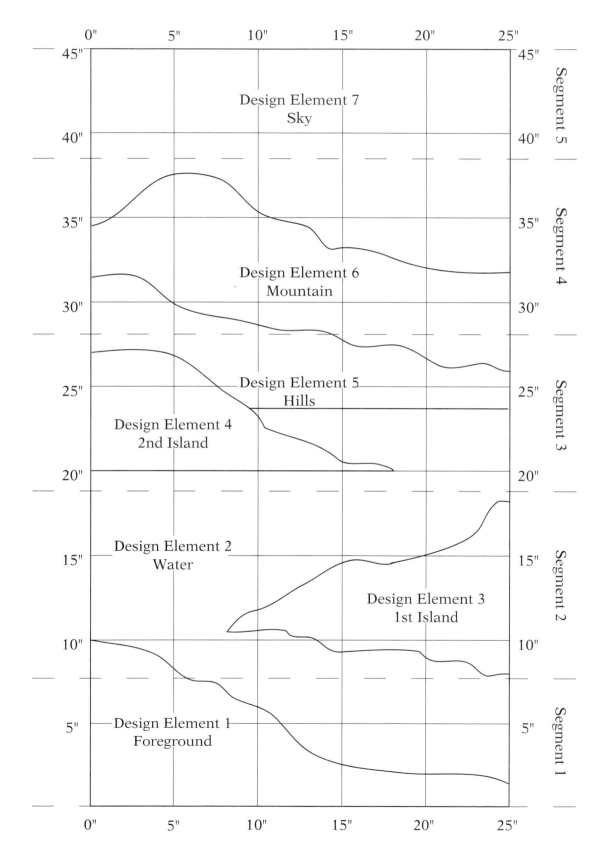

4. Country Hills

Size: 36" wide by 48" high

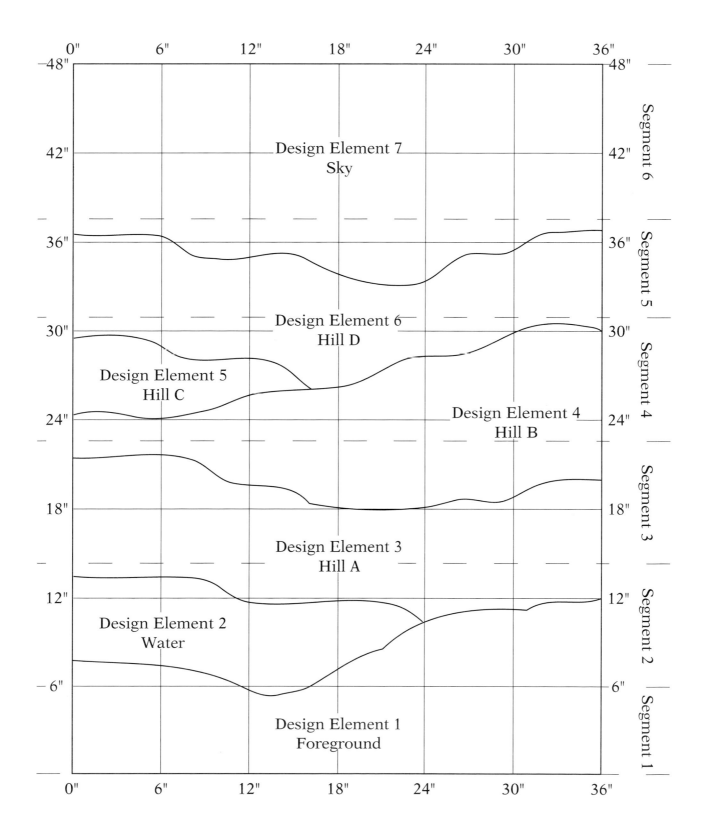

Design Element 7
Sky

Design Element 6
Hill D

Design Element 5
Hill C

Design Element 4
Hill B

Design Element 3
Hill A

Design Element 2
Water

Design Element 1
Foreground

Segment 6
Segment 5
Segment 4
Segment 3
Segment 2
Segment 1

5. Going Home

Size: 35" wide by 28" high

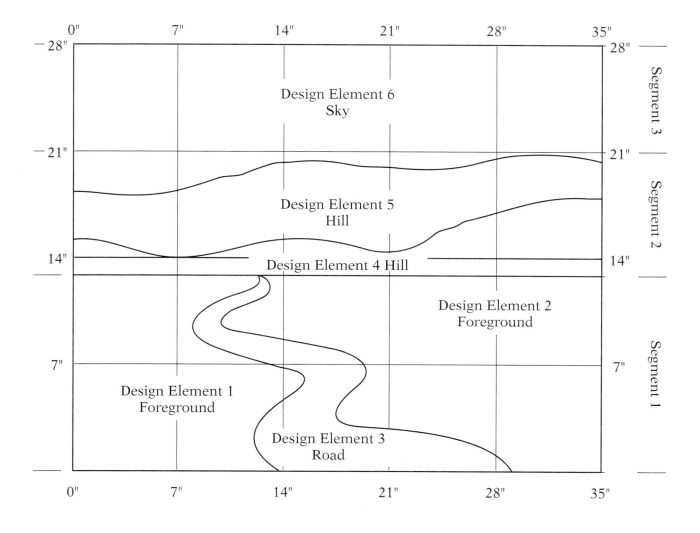

6. Mountain Reflection

Size: 21" wide by 49" high

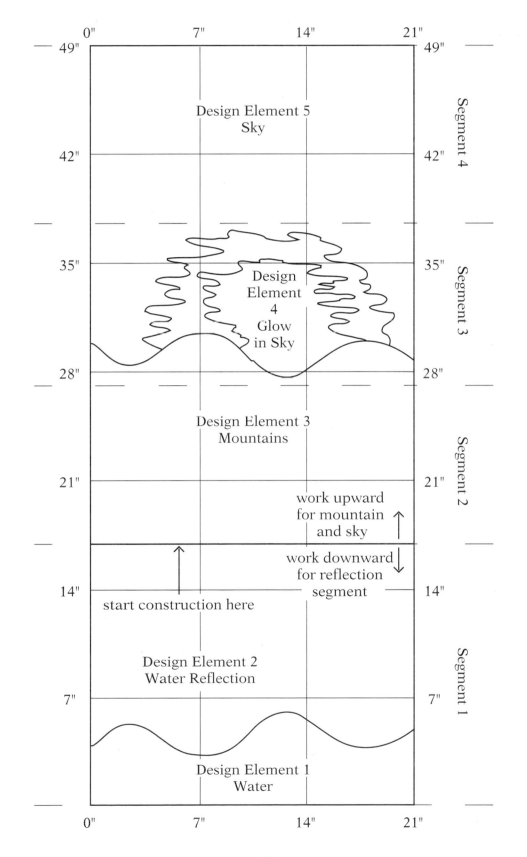

7. *Hawaiian Memory*

Size: 48" wide by 24" high

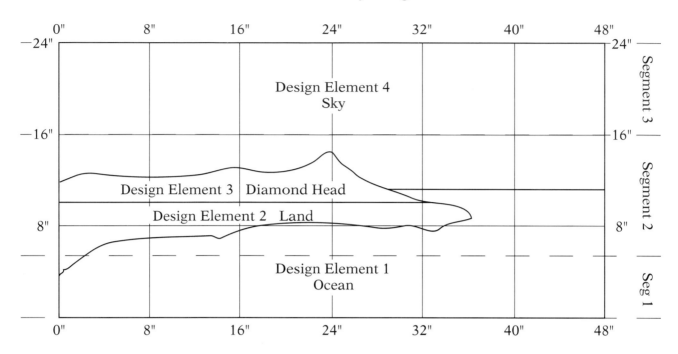

8. *Distant Hills*

Size: 30" wide by 18" high

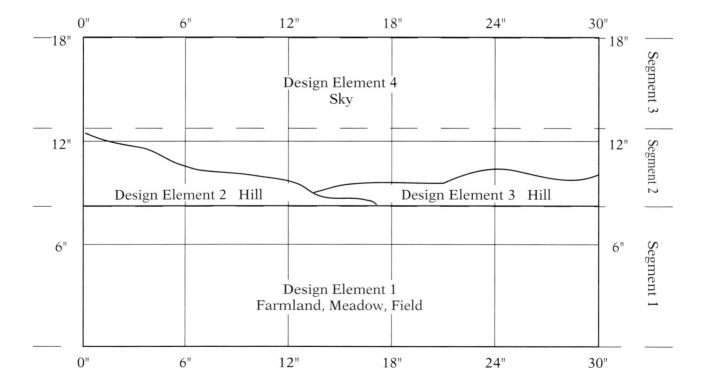

9. Memories of Waterton

Size: 70" wide by 45" high

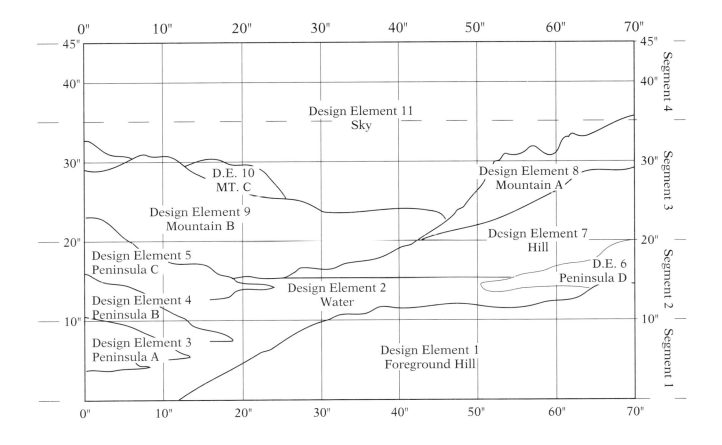

10. Repose

Size: 51" wide by 34" high

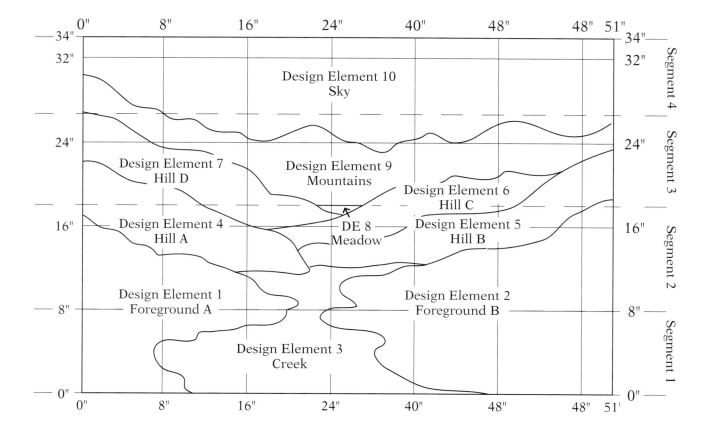

PART SIX:

In Conclusion

Landscapes & Illusions has given me the opportunity to share with you the valuable learning experiences that I have had exploring color, illusions, and techniques while creating fabric landscapes. It is my hope that you will find yourself as fascinated with creating scenic pictures as I have been. In the future I look forward to seeing many magnificent fabric landscapes which reflect the beauty of our environment.

Feel free to expand on the ideas and methods presented in this book. By doing so, you will strengthen, enhance, and refine the landscape artform and strip piecing techniques that have been presented. May this book also give you the incentive to challenge your own imagination in fiber and open the doors to further creative expression.

As you search, risk, and explore, remember that each work of art is not meant to be a masterpiece, but rather a stopping-off point along the quiet, unmarked pathway to lifelong creativity.

Accent Color
An accent color is a hue that has a minor role within a work of art. It is the least dominant of all the colors used.

Afterimages
When you stare intensely at a color, a new hue will come into view. It will surround or float above the first color. This second color is called an afterimage. Each color has its own afterimage partnership.

Back, Backing, Backing Material
When a landscape picture is completed, the back-side of the construction will be covered with a backing material. If you plan to quilt your landscape, this backing material will be the bottom layer of the three sections.

Baste, Basting, Basting Stitches
A basting stitch temporarily holds two or more fabric layers together. Very large running stitches are used in basting. In preparation for quilting, the landscape top, batting, and backing are basted together.

Batting   *Synonym: Wadding*
Batting is polyester, cotton, wool, or a blend of fibers that is wadded together for a stuffing. The uses and look of batting vary. In quilting, thin batting is placed between the finished top and the backing material. After the three layers are basted together, a design is marked on the top layer. Then, by hand or machine, the three layers are sewn together with quilting stitches. The combination of stitches and batting add depth and interest to the surface design.

Binding
The binding finishes the fiber piece by enclosing the raw edges around the perimeter. Several different techniques can be used to complete this process.

Borders
Borders are additional bands of fabric design that can be attached to the landscape picture after it is completed. When used, borders should enhance the scenic design.

Color Family
A color family represents the range of colors within a specific hue. Examples of color families include blue, green, orange, and yellow. Each of these families incorporates many hues within its range.

Color Illusions   *See Visual Illusions*

Color Scales
Color scales play a role similar to scales in music. They simply give fundamental order to the various elements of color. Color scales are broken into four major divisions: pure hues, tints, shades, and tones. Within each scale there can be a countless series of ascending and descending colors. The specific interval between hues within a scale can vary, depending on the artist's needs.

Color Wheel
A color wheel is simply an organized sequence of pure colors traditionally arranged within a circular format. Although there are several noted color wheels, artists generally use the (Herbert E.) Ives Color Circle as their color wheel source. This particular color wheel deals with pigments and dyes, as well as the visual order of pure colors. The primary colors of this pigment color wheel are yellow, magenta, and cyan (turquoise).

Construction Drawing
A construction drawing is the graph paper design that you use as a guide while creating your fabric landscape picture. The construction drawing contains your design, a color plan, grid lines, incremental measurements, segment markings, and in some cases, prospective quilting lines.

Design Element

Design elements are the different pictorial features in your drawing and landscape picture. Each design element has its own color and fabric selection. For instance, a mountain, a hill, a lake, the sky, and a flower garden are separate design elements.

Dominant Color

A dominant color is the hue that is most visually present in an artwork. Every work of art should have a dominant color to be visually successful.

Field

The entire background area of a design is considered the field. This term is used primarily when discussing whether the background needs to be shaded or toned to attain a specific visual illusion.

Figure-8 Pinning

A figure-8 pinning is a type of pinning used when you need temporarily to attach a thread securely to a pin that is already positioned on the fabric. Although its greatest use is for gathering basting threads, the figure-8 pinning is invaluable during the straightening process.

Highlights

A brilliantly lit area within a picture is called a highlight. It entails extreme brightness. Sunlight that flows onto an object within a scene is a highlight.

Horizontal

Any line or object that is parallel to the horizon is horizontal. The upper and lower edges of your landscape picture are on horizontal planes or lines.

Horizontal Plumb Line

For straightening purposes, the strongest horizontal strip in your landscape becomes the horizontal reference. Using this strip as a reference point, the upper and lower horizontal plumb lines are established. From these two lines, the upper and lower finished edges of your landscape are marked and cut.

Hue

In this book, hue is used in its broadest sense. A hue is a color. Yellow and orange are hues.

Illusions   *See Visual Illusions*

Intensity

Intensity refers to the vividness or the relative pureness of gray within a color. A color that has no gray in it has strong intensity. Colors which are made with large amounts of gray added to them have weak intensity. For example, the color rose has weak intensity because it contains a great deal of gray. Magenta, however, is of strong intensity because it is devoid of gray.

Luminosity (Luminous)

Luminosity is the ability to glow from within. The sun, a light bulb, and a candle flame are examples of luminosity because they all emit self-generated light.

Luster

Luster is reflected light, rather than self-generated light. Light falling onto a lake is an example of luster. The resulting reflected light can be soft, brilliant, or glossy.

Perpendicular

When a line is perpendicular to another line, it is at right angles (90 degrees) to the other. When straightening a landscape, make certain that your vertical and horizontal edges are perpendicular to each other. To establish accuracy, use a T square.

Plumb Line
Straightening Technique (*modified*)

An actual plumb line establishes true vertical by suspending a weight on a line. With modifications, we can straighten or make vertical the sides of our fabric art by using a modified plumb line made from thread. The plumb line that we use has no weight, however. The line is made from top-stitching thread.

Pure Colors

Primary colors and all colors formed by their mixture are pure colors. There is no black, white, or gray present in pure colors. Pure colors are intense and vibrant. They represent the colors of summer.

Quilting

Quilting is the process of stitching three layers of fiber together: the top, the inner batting (wadding), and the backing fabric. Together they form an interlocking sandwich when quilted. As well, it is possible to quilt the top and backing together without using any batting. Besides adding strength to the work, the quilting stitches add linear surface design and visual depth. Quilting can be done by hand or machine.

Reference Points

Reference points are specific places on two adjacent fabric strips where the design elements need to be matched precisely. When attaching one horizontal strip to the next adjoining strip, sew the two in position at the specific reference points using the V pinning method.

Root Color

A root color is the original hue within a specified group of colors. If you were blending the color teal with its afterimage, apricot, teal would be considered the root color.

Secondary Color

A secondary color is one that plays a smaller visual role than the dominant color. However, a secondary color is more important and more visible than any color other than the dominant hue, including accent colors.

Segment

Segments are divisions in your drawing that are used during the construction process to ease sewing and to avoid overhandling of the sewn strips. Segments are not equal in size; the division lines are placed where you think it will be easiest to separate the strips during construction. Segment lines are marked on the construction drawing with horizontal dashes.

Shades

A shade is a color that has had black added to it. Shades are always darker than the pure color from which they are derived. Shades can be autumnal and should be used for all scenes that represent the fall season. They also are used for night scenes, or when the effect of dimness or darkness is desired.

Staystitch, Staystitching

A staystitch is a stitch used to keep fabrics from stretching or fraying. It is also used to stabilize all sides of each completed segment. The staystitch seam is sewn just inside the seam allowance so that it cannot be seen after the final stitching has been completed.

Strip

A strip is a piece of fabric that has been cut from yardage, generally widthwise. It is cut to a predeter-mined width, which is calculated by deciding the desired finished width of a fabric strip, plus two ¼ inch seam allowances. (Example: ¾" finished width + ½" seam allowance [¼" + ¼"] = a cut strip of 1¼" width.)

Strip Set

A strip set is a combination of two or more strips which have been sewn together vertically. Strip sets are eventually made into larger sections called segments.

T Square

A T square is an invaluable tool for many construction and finishing procedures where accuracy is extremely important. The T square is used for determining perpendicular and parallel lines. It is a straight edge or ruler that has a perpendicular crosspiece at one end. A wooden 24-inch-long T square is an excellent, reasonably priced choice. In use, the lip of the crossbar fits on the edge of a table, counter, breadboard, or other straight edge. When it is in position, the T square establishes a marking or cutting line. (T squares may be bought at art, architecture, and school supply stores.)

Tints

A tint is a color that has had white added to it. Tints are always lighter than the pure color from which they are derived. Tints represent the season of spring. They should be used with scenes which involve delicate colorations.

Tones

Tones are colors which have had gray added to them. They can be light, medium, or dark in coloration. Tones are used in winter scenes because these hues exude a wintry effect. They are also used to give the illusion of fog, haze, or mist.

V Pinning

Reference points are joined by using the V pinning method. One pin is thrust through both fabric strips at a precise point. (It is not actually pinned, but just pushed through the two pieces of fabric at an exact location.) Two other pins are then pinned on either side of the first, forming a V. This V pinning stabilizes the reference point pin.

Value

Value describes the relative lightness of a color toward white, or the relative darkness of a color toward black. A light color has high value, while a dark color has low value. Value has to do with how much light is reflected from a color. The lighter the color, the more light is reflected; the darker the color, the more light is absorbed. Pink is high in value, whereas navy blue has low value.

Vertex
The vertex is the exact point at which the two sides of an angle intersect or meet.

Vertical
A vertical line, or object, is perpendicular to the horizon; it is at right angles to a horizontal line. The left and right sides of your straightened landscape picture are vertical; their lines are perpendicular to the upper and lower edges of the picture.

Vertical Plumb Line
For straightening purposes, you need to establish a vertical plumb line on your landscape in order to make the sides of your textile art perpendicular. This perpendicular line is placed near the horizontal midpoint of your picture. With a T square, other tools, and your lower horizontal plumb line as a reference point, this vertical plumb line can be located. After the vertical plumb line has been established, the left and right side plumb lines can be found.

Visual Balance
Visual balance is the sense of harmony between the design and the colors within a picture. As a partnership, the two elements are seen as one when visual balance has been achieved. If this delicate balance has not been realized, either the design or portions of the coloration pull out and distract the viewer. To achieve visual balance with color, you should have a dominant color and a variation of values.

Visual Depth
Visual depth is attained by the effective use of color. When used successfully, the art no longer looks flat, but takes on an added dimension of depth. When visual depth has been achieved, the viewer has a sense of being present within the landscape. Depth perception and three-dimensional color are other terms used for visual depth.

Visual Illusions
Visual illusions, or color illusions, are perceptions within artwork that are created through the use of color placement. These illusions trick our minds into believing that we see an image that does not actually exist. A picture showing depth, the glowing of the sun, or the moon's luster on snow are all examples of visual illusions—ideas created by using color effectively.

Appendix II:
Bibliography

Birren, Faber. *Color Perception in Art.* West Chester, Pennsylvania: Shiffer Publishing Ltd., 1986.

_____. *Creative Color.* New York: Van Nostrand Reinhold Company, 1961.

Itten, Johannes. *The Elements of Color.* New York: Van Nostrand Reinhold Company, 1970.

Leman, Bonnie, ed. *Quilter's Newsletter Magazine: Pieced Pictures.* Wheatridge, Colorado: Leman Publications, Inc., pp. 24-26, June, 1986.

Morris, William, Editor. *The American Heritage Dictionary of the English Language.* Boston: Houghton Mifflin Co., 1981.

Ocvirk, Otto, Robert Robert, Robert E. Stinson, and Phillip R. Wigg. *Art Fundamentals Theory and Practice.* Dubuque, Iowa: William C. Brown Co., Publishers, 1968.

Sargent, Walter. *The Enjoyment and Use of Color.* New York: Dover Publications, Inc., 1964.

Suggested Reading List

Beyer, Jinny. *Patchwork Patterns.* McLean, Virginia: EPM Publications, Inc., 1979. **(excellent; traditional block designs, basic pattern drafting)**

Gutcheon, Beth. *The Perfect Patchwork Primer.* Baltimore: Penquin Books Inc., 1974. **(history and basics of traditional quiltmaking)**

Hassel, Carla. *Super Quilter II.* Des Moines, Iowa: Wallace-Homestead Book Company, 1982. **(extensive information about basic quiltmaking techniques)**

James, Michael. *The Quiltmaker's Handbook.* Englewood Cliffs, New Jersey: Prentice-Hall, Inc., 1978. **(excellent book; thorough coverage of traditional quiltmaking techniques with present day quiltmakers in mind)**

_____. *The Second Quiltmaker's Handbook.* Englewood Cliffs, New Jersey: Prentice-Hall, Inc., 1981. **(excellent; addresses contemporary quilts as art: design, techniques, and color)**

McClun, Diana and Nownes, Laura. *Quilts! Quilts!! Quilts!!! The Complete Guide to Quiltmaking.* San Francisco: The Quilt Digest Press, 1988. **(excellent reference for beginning quiltmaking)**

Wong, Wucius. *Principles of Color Design.* New York: Van Nostrand Reinhold, 1987. **(elementary design and color principles)**

_____. *Principles of Two-Dimensional Design.* New York: Van Nostrand Reinhold Company, 1972. **(excellent coverage of design principles)**

Periodicals:

American Quilter, American Quilter's Society, Division of Schroeder Publishing Co., Inc., 5801 Kentucky Dam Road, Paducah, Kentucky, 42001

Quilter's Newsletter Magazine, Leman Publications, Inc., Box 394, Wheatridge, Colorado 80034

Sources

Hand-dyed fabrics, quilt stores, and other offerings

Below is a listing of hand-dyed fabric companies that have mail order services.

Alaska Dyeworks
300 West Swanson, Suite 101
Wasilla, Alaska 99687

Clemmensen Fiber Design
9797 E. Bullard Avenue
Clovis, California 93612

Lunn Fabrics
922 Madison Street
Denver, Colorado 80206

Shades
2880 Holcomb Bridge Rd, Suite b-9
Alpharetta, Georgia 30201

Skydyes
83 Richmond Lane
West Hartford, Connecticut 06117

True Colors
Rd. 3, Box 91, Wood Road
Pittstown, New Jersey 08867

Below is a small portion of the innumerable stores which are recognized for their outstanding offerings of fabric, speciality items, and/or boutique merchandise. Due to limited space, it is not possible to make this list comprehensive. Check a quilting directory for a complete guide.

Cotton Patch
1025 Brown Ave.
Lafayette, California 94549

Country Quilt & Fabric
230 N. Main Street
Rutland, Vermont 05701

Double T Quilt Shop
219 Berkshire Avenue
Springfield, Massachusetts 01107

G Street Fabrics
11854 Rockville Pike
Rockville, Maryland 20852

The Glass Thimble
3434 N. High Street
Columbus, Ohio 43214

Great Expectations
14520 Memorial Drive #54
Houston, Texas 77079

In The Beginning
8201 Lake City Way N.E.
Seattle, Washington 98115

Joseph's Coat
26 Main Street
Peterborough, New Hampshire
03458

Osage County Quilt Factory
400 Walnut Street
Overbrook, Kansas 66524-0490

The Quilt Box at Walnut Springs
Farm
Warsaw Road (Hwy. 467)
Dry Ridge, Kentucky 41035

Quilters' Paradise
339 Pollasky
Clovis, California 93612

Stitchin' Post
106 Cascade
Sisters, Oregon 97759

Write for a free catalog of other fine quilting books from C&T Publishing, P.O. Box 1456, Lafayette, CA 94549

About The Author

Like most women, Joen Wolfrom has many varied roles. She alternates between artist, quiltmaker, teacher, lecturer, writer, mother, wife, homemaker, private school board member, president of a small greeting card corporation, and advocate for excellent education for all students.

Having been an elementary classroom teacher, a teacher of learning disabled students, and a teacher/consultant for gifted education, the entire educational spectrum continues to be an important interest of Joen's. She remains active in the educational community.

In her artistic endeavors, Joen enjoys creating site-specific commissioned art, and finds most of her time committed to these projects. For her, commission work offers interesting design assignments and unique challenges. She also enjoys color, design, and technical exploration with fabric, and appreciates the opportunity to share her ideas through teaching and lecturing.

Joen resides with her husband and three children on Fox Island, a rural 3200-acre community in Washington State's southern Puget Sound. This pastoral setting offers continual opportunities to observe the colorful beauty of nature that is often reflected in her landscape art.

Inquiries about greeting cards of selected artworks by the author may be addressed to Bon Bluff Images, Inc., 104 Bon Bluff, Fox Island, WA 98333. Send LSASE. Inquiries concerning current workshops and lectures by the author may be sent to the same address.